Preach On!

J. Alfred Smith

BROADMAN PRESS
Nashville, Tennessee

Library of Congress Cataloging in Publication Data

Smith, J. Alfred (James Alfred)
   Preach on!

   Bibliography: p.
   1. Preaching.   I. Title.
BV4211.2.S63   1984   251   84-9439
ISBN 0-8054-2112-2

To

J. Alfred Smith, Jr. and Paul Rigmaiden, son and son-in-law, two able young preachers; to each of my children in the gospel ministry; and with affection to my peer in preaching, T. L. Willis, who pushes me to continue in pursuit of excellence

Acknowledgments

Many excellent books appear at the book stores on preaching. Why should another book appear which may never be considered an excellent book on preaching? This is the risk any author must take who dares place his or her thoughts into writing. However, few attempts have been made to write on preaching as a poetic art form. Fewer attempts have been made to write about the style of the Black preacher.

Current books on preaching address the issues of exegesis, exposition, correct outlining of the sermon, communication theory, homiletical construction, law and gospel, and the theological content of the sermon. Scholars have written about the preacher in dialogue with his text and the preacher in dialogue with the congregation. Attention has been given to preaching as counseling and the relationship of preaching to worship, as well as the preaching event.

The purpose of this handbook is to share with the reader some acceptable norms for developing an effective preaching style and to illustrate how some respected preachers have used these norms within the classical tradition of Black preaching. Much of the material comes from the struggles, failures, and continuing education of the author in his painful pursuit of learning by listening to great preaching and by attempting to preach acceptably at the Allen Temple Baptist Church of Oakland, California. This material is not the final word of preaching style; but it has been shared at the American Baptist Seminary of the West in Berkeley, California, and at Golden Gate Baptist Theological Seminary in Mill Valley, California, in preaching classes. The encouragement to explore style in preaching came from Dr. William Malcolmson when he invited me to lecture at Linfield College, McMinnville, Oregon, for the Continuing Education School for Pastors of the Western States in 1978. Since then, Dr. William Pinson, who coauthored with Dr. Clyde Fant the multivolumed *Centuries of Great Preaching,* has allowed me to share some of these insights in the annual Doctor of Ministry Seminar on Proclamation and Worship.

I am deeply indebted to Dean W. Morgan Patterson of Golden Gate Seminary; Dr. Sidney Smith of The Sunday School Board of the Southern Baptist Convention; President L. Doward McBain of Berkeley; and William Pinson, former president of Golden Gate Seminary for encouraging me to grow as a preacher. I am indebted to my friend, Bill Malcolmson, who has written a widely used text called *The Preaching Event,* for introducing me to style in preaching as an area of lifelong study; and to my wife, JoAnna Smith, for her criticisms, companionship, and support. Aramis Fouche loaned me his summer vacation home so I could write without distraction. Thanks be to him.

Mr. Clayton L. Anderson is a long-time friend. He has detected mistakes and corrected them and typed several drafts of the manuscript, just as he did when he typed seminar papers, earlier manuscripts, and my doctoral thesis for Golden Gate Baptist Theological Seminary. I owe him a large debt of gratitude.

W. Somerset Maugham, speaking of style in authors of secular acclaim, could be speaking about style in preaching:

> And yet we know how fatal the pursuit of liveliness may be: it may result in the tiresome acrobatics of Meredith. Macaulay and Carlyle were in their different ways arresting; but at the heavy cost of naturalness. Their flashy effects destroy their persuasiveness;

you would not believe a man was very intent on ploughing a furrow if he carried a hoop with him and jumped through it at every other step. A good style should show no sign of effort.[1]

J. ALFRED SMITH, SR.
November, 1983

Note

1. James Douglas Robertson, *Handbook of Preaching Resources from Literature* (Grand Rapids, Michigan: Baker Book House, 1962), pp. 425-426.

Special Endorsements

Dr. J. Alfred Smith, Sr., is a lover of preaching, as well as a learned practitioner of this art which, at its best, must rank with the noblest arts of them all. Dr. Smith has delved deeply and skillfully into the styles of proclamation which characterize some of the most widely heard preachers of our time.

He examines with remarkable discernment the drum beat, flutes, trumpets, and violins to be heard in words and how they send mental messages and stir emotions as old as humanity. The writer's reverence for God and respect for our mortal plight prevent his treatment of this essentially sacred undertaking from descending to the level of advice on manipulative technique.

This book will be treasured by students of the preaching craft and will be helpful to those who find solace and strength in hearing earnest, inspired preaching. Teachers of preaching will undoubtedly discover that this is the missing textbook which the discipline of homiletics has needed so long. People can be taught *how* to preach, but it is doubtful they can be taught to preach. *Preach On!* comes close to doing both.

Dr. Gardner C. Taylor, pastor
Concord Baptist Church of Christ
Brooklyn, New York

Since 1965, I have been a teacher of preachers, both in seminary and continuing education events. Over the years, I had developed my own style, both in teaching preachers and in my own preaching. In the last eight years, I have experienced a revitalization in my preaching. This has been due, primarily, to a growing number of opportunities to preach in Black churches, as well as exposure to great Black preachers. Dr. J. Alfred Smith, Sr., is one of those persons who has given me such an opportunity. I am deeply grateful to him for his gift to me.

In recent years, it has become increasingly possible for all persons to learn from the Black experience in the area of preaching. I think of books by Dr. Henry Mitchell and Dr. Gardner Taylor. We are all the richer for their contributions. And now comes along another one who is a multi-cultural person, a citizen of many worlds, who communicates across racial and class lines in a unique and profoundly Christian manner —Dr. J. Alfred Smith, Sr.

Dr. Smith has been acting dean of our institution, a full-status professor of parish ministry, a field supervisor for both M.Div. and D.Min. students, and an advisor and confidant of faculty, students, and administration. The most important thing I can say about Dr. Smith is—to borrow one of his favorite phrases—"he is my teacher." When you read *Preach On!* he will become your teacher as well. I commend him, his insights, his example, and his conviction to you.

Dr. WILLIAM L. MALCOLMSON, vice-president
  and dean of academic affairs
American Baptist Seminary of the West
Berkeley, California

Contents

1. Styles of Preaching 15
   A Definition of Style • Three Basic Factors for Acquiring an Effective Preaching Style • Enriching the Three Basic Factors of Preaching Style • Origin of Words • Shades of Meaning of Words • The Study of Word Choice
2. The Study of Poetic Diction 23
   The Rules of Poetic Diction • Skillful Use of Poetic Diction by Black Preachers • Contrasting Poetic Diction with Prose Diction
3. The Use of Figures of Speech 28
   Metaphor • Synecdoche • Hyperbole • Personification • Apostrophe • Exclamation • Interrogation • Antithesis • Epigram • Climax • Repetition • Contrast • Elegance • Quotations
4. The Use of the Voice in Developing Your Preaching Style 34
   The Relationship of the Voice to Preaching Style • The Preaching Voice as a Musical Instrument • The Four Vocal Mechanisms of Preaching • Proper Breathing
5. Sermon Arrangement and Style 40
   Sentence Structure • Paragraph Construction • Transitional Sentences • Sermon Titles • Introduction • Body • Conclusion
6. A Theology of Preaching 47
Bibliography 55

Appendix 1. Some Contemporary Preaching Styles
Worthy of Observation and Study 60
Appendix 2. Guidelines for Interpreting a Text 64
Appendix 3. Criteria for Evaluating a Sermon 66
Appendix 4. A Course Outline for Creativity in Black
Preaching, J. Alfred Smith, Sr. 68
Appendix 5. Examples of Written Styles of Preaching by
Students at American Baptist Seminary of
the West 71
Christ Asks for a Verdict, Tobina A. Dal-
ton • The Feast of Christ the King, Rob-
ert Lee McCree • Curiosity Is a Function
of Jesus, Robert J. Thomas • The Gift of
the Two Mites, Roland S. Ruffin • The
Danger in Listening to the Devil, Albert
C. Coleman • A Question for You, Jesus!
Ron Martin Dent • She Hath Done What
She Couldn't, David Bunje
Appendix 6. Examples of Written Styles of Preaching by
Students at Allen Temple Baptist Church
.... 95
Terminal Indifference, Paul Q.Rigmaiden
• What's Your Story? Jini Robinson • To
the Church at Smyrna: "Hold On!" Eu-
gene Williams • Persistence Rewarded,
Haywood Harvey • The Most Dangerous
People in the Church, Robert K. Gordon
Appendix 7. Examples of Oratory and Style in Modern
Black Preachers 115
Songs of Hope from Dungeons of De-
spair, J. Alfred Smith, Jr. • A Message
Which Helped to Shape a Life, Charles
Satchell Morris, II

Preach On!

1
Styles of Preaching

A Definition of Style

Style is the manner in which a speaker uses language in expressing thought. Sometimes great ideas fail to reach an audience because the style of the message lacks skillful and artistic expression. Plain speech offers dignity, power, and beauty to the message. An effective pulpit presentation should be free from crudeness and coarseness of language. Since the preacher is one who dares to speak for God, only the best possible language should be utilized. The use of language reveals not only the beauty or ugliness of an idea but also is an indication of the nature of the speaker's personality.

Style is the uniqueness of the preacher's way of communication. Style is the mirror of the thought and thought forms of the preacher. The personality, natural mental gifts, training, and cultural tastes are components which constitute style. Nevertheless, a person can improve upon style by studying grammar, logic, rhetoric, and English composition. The writer of this manuscript painfully plods along almost daily in pursuit of excellence in these technical skills which produce beauty and clarity of style. Three factors which seem to be basic to the acquiring of an effective style are thought, audience, and sincerity.

Three Basic Factors for Acquiring an Effective Preaching Style

The speaker should have something worthwhile to say. Skill in the transmission of verbal symbolism is of no avail if the speaker has no message. The one who speaks for God has a message of ultimate worth. It is necessary for the messenger to master the message. Too much ornament can overdress the style so that the audience misses the message.

The audience must always be kept in mind. To whom are you speaking? and how well read are they? are important questions. What kind of language must you use to effectively communicate with them? A professional paper is in order when appearing before seminarians and professors. They will understand the technical language of seminary studies. Critical hearers who are nonseminary trained will desire logical and precise expression. Average audiences prefer the concrete words to the abstract and the familiar words to the technical. But all audiences demand sincerity.

Sincerity of presentation means being honest in thought and delivery. The ideas given in a message should flow from the conviction level of the speaker. Though the preacher may have doubts, the sermon is no place for those doubts to be aired. Preaching must always be a persuasive presentation. In influencing the audience to accept the message, no imitation of other effective speakers and no subprofessional circus-like antics should be employed because this kind of behavior is devoid of sincerity and promotes sensationalism.

Enriching the Three Basic
Factors of Preaching Style

Thought, audience, and sincerity are three basic factors for acquiring an effective style. Each speaker can improve the quality of speaking style by enriching the three basic factors with systematic, varied reading of good literature, including notable speeches. Such reading will make clear the differences between written and oral style. Speech style makes greater use of interpolations, asides, editorial comments, personal pronouns in the first or second person, interrogatives, contractions, broken sentences, and repetition. The language of written prose differs from good oral style. A study of excellent literature challenges the preacher to improve personal standards. *Roget's Thesaurus,* with its array of synonyms, and an up-to-date dictionary, which provides a record of current usage, belong on every speaker's bookshelf. An excellent rule of preaching is to cultivate daily an appetite for the study of words.

An effective student of preaching will taste words with the sensitivity of a gourmet who is an authority on the location of the best restaurants in town. The student will select verbs carefully. Whenever possible the use of the verb to be will be sparsely used. Most of the time it should be used to create a pensive or pondering mood. For example:

> God is our refuge and strength (Ps. 46:1).
> The Lord is my light and my salvation; whom shall
> I fear? (Ps. 27:1).

Assertion verbs are more potent and pungent than the verb *to be.* Here are a few: *enrich, enhance, constitutes, undergirds, implies, fortifies,* and *motivates.*

Dynamic verbs are most effective for creating vibrancy and vitality. Notice the effect of the following:

> A loveless heart *eroded* by hatred
> His voice *thundered*
> The child *stormed* out of the classroom
> Fear *froze* the hearts of the disciples

Be careful of redundancy or the unnecessary repetition of words. Sometimes this is called tautology. Examples of tautology are: learning disciples; volumes of books; biography of Paul's life.

Some words have similar meanings but are not interchangeable, such as *affect* and *effect; arbitrate* and *mediate; illusion* and *allusion; climax* and *conclusion;* and *generous* and *gracious.* Some terms are pronounced exactly alike but have different meanings, such as *alter* and *altar; gait* and *gate; principle* and *principal; capitol* and *capital; complement* and *compliment; raise* and *raze;* and *rite, right,* and *write.*

Origin of Words

As you know, a large part of English vocabulary has its origin in Latin. In understanding English better, one should become acquainted with Latin roots. Let your attention center upon the English word *animal* which comes from the Latin *anima*. In Latin, *anima* means life, breath, soul, or spirit. So from the Latin stem *anim*, a number of English words were born: *animalcule*, a tiny live thing; *animate*, to breathe life into; *equanimity*, equal; *magnanimous*, of large or noble spirit; *unanimous*, one mind; *inanimate*, without life; *animosity*, enmity; *pusillanimous*, coward; and *animadvert*, to turn the mind to, to criticize. Look now at the stem of *magnus* which in English means large: *magnate*, an important person in business or industry; *magnify*, to make large; *magnificence*, splendor, grandeur, great or greatness; *magniloquent*, speaking in big terms of oratory or flowery language; *magnitude*, big or great; and *magnum opus*, a great or important literary work.

The preacher would do well to study the Latin stems of words now used in conversational English. This study will reap the rich rewards in speaking which the pianist derives from a daily and disciplined practice of scales in music. Such an exercise with the word *benevolence* would reveal: *bene* (well) *volens* (wishing), which means wishing others well. Every church has a deacons' or benevolence fund used to assist the poor and needy. *Bene* is also found in other words that the preacher will need in his or her vocabulary, such as *benefit, beneficiary, benediction,* and *benefactor.* Every preacher has to use the stem of *volens,* which in English means wishing, *volition, voluntary, volunteer.*

Every preacher uses the word *benediction.* The word comes from two Latin stems: *bene* (well) and *dicere* (to tell or to say), hence, benediction literally means to say well, or saying well. The studious preacher cannot help but be intrigued with the word *benefactor* (*facere,* to do or make; *bene,* well), hence, benefactor means well doer. From the stem of *facere* the following English words emerge: *factor, factory, manufacture, fact, factotum,* and *factual.*

Other interesting word studies in Latin are *signa* and *portare.* From *signa* (sign), we get such words as *sign, insignia, signify, design, signature,* and *insignificant.* From porta (to carry), we get such words as *porter, portable, reporter, deport, import,* and *export.*

The preacher who is serious about becoming a master of spoken English should have an elementary introduction to Greek stems, as well as the most commonly used ones in Latin. Learning these stems need not be painful. It can become a hobby. The preacher may make a scrapbook for the weekly enrichment of his or her vocabulary. Let the student now take a look at the Greek word *monos,* for one. From *monos* (one), we get the following words: *monocle,* a glass for one eye; *monogamy,* one marriage; *monotheism,* one God; *monotone,* speaking in one tone; *monologue,* speech of one person; and *monosyllable,* a word of one syllable.

Because the meaning of words change, the preacher should read current literature on word usage and consult the dictionary for acceptable English terminology. More than three hundred years ago, many English words meant just the opposite of what they mean in today's world. Old English *stink* referred to any odor at all and *amusing* meant amazing, and *villain* was applied to one who worked in a villa, and a *hussy* was a housewife.

The study of the Bible also requires the preacher to be sensitive to idioms and patterns of thought that are not germane to current language practices. The average preacher may harm the honor of those who translated the King James Bible; and he or she may do violence to those Scriptures if the preacher is not aware of the changes that have taken place in the English language since the King James Version of the Bible was written. For example, in King James' English, *conversation* meant conduct, *ghost* meant spirit, *purchase a good degree* meant to gain a good standing, and *prevent* meant to precede, and *all* meant allow. Some three hundred English words in the King James Version of the Bible are substantially different from what those words now convey. The student of preaching who is not a student of biblical Hebrew and Greek can obtain the help that is needed in correct word interpretation by using some of the most recent translations and research and resource materials at reputable Bible book stores. Professors in local seminaries are eager to discuss with persons the interpretations of the Scriptures.

Because language is constantly changing, the ever-learning student of preaching may find invaluable assistance from reading the monthly issues of *Reader's Digest.* This author has discovered pleasure and new knowledge from reading the following articles in *Reader's Digest:* "Toward Picturesque Speech," "It Pays to Enrich Your Word Power," "Points to Ponder," and "All in a Day's Work."

Those who can afford it should read materials like *The Atlantic Monthly, The Saturday Review of Literature,* and editorial comments of persons who write for major newspapers as well as magazines, such as *Time* and *Newsweek.* The major television news persons work very hard to be excellent models of correctness in the use of spoken English.

In the study of language, the student is concerned about the origin of words. The shades of meaning and the changes in the meanings of words are very important things to know. The emotional meaning of words in a specific cultural setting or before a particular audience and the possible images words can conjure in the minds of the audience are matters which should claim the attention of each person who studies style in speaking. Words have color, size, weight, feeling, force, movement, sound, smell, taste, and touch. Words can express anger, anxiety, contempt, disappointment, fear, gratitude, grief, hate, hope, jealousy, joy, love, pity, and pride. Learning the mastery of words helps to determine not so much the content as the style of the message. As the artist skillfully uses paints, pigments, and brushes, so does the preacher use language to paint, prove, and persuade the hearers.

Shades of Meaning of Words

The study of language enables the preacher to use words with the same selectivity as a trained singer. The pitch, key, and tone with which notes are sung or words are expressed create the mood of acceptance or rejection. The way a word or a combination of words is used can motivate an audience to behave as a mob or to be as pliable as putty to the verbal invitations of the preacher. Therefore, the power of the message is influenced by the manner in which the message is presented. Clear, convincing communication employed by the selectivity of a sensitive and trained spokesperson constitutes a combination of skill in word choice and the artistic articulation of vocabulary in the delivery of the sermon. The study of word choice is called diction.

The Study of Word Choice

There are rules which determine literary excellence. The proper use of these rules will enable the speaker or writer to develop skill in both prose and poetic diction. Some of these rules are:

1. In the choice of words, let the paramount consideration be exactness.
2. Seek to have at command more than one expression for the same thing.
3. Cultivate the habit of observing the derivation and history of words.
4. Enlarge your vocabulary by diligent study of usage by the best writers.
5. Beware of words too new to have a recognized place in the language.
6. Be sure of ample justification before coining new formations or compounds.
7. Be suspicious of current newspaper and colloquial terms.
8. Do not, out of mere affectation, indulge an ancient word or archaic term foreign to the background of your audience.
9. Do not employ words peculiar to a limited section of the country unless you are speaking in that region and are confident that you will not insult the hearers by using those words.
10. Do not use technical terms where they are not likely to be understood.
11. Do not use an unnaturalized foreign word unless you are

sure it expresses an idea for which there are no fitting terms in English.

12. Use no expression thoughtlessly.

13. Avoid the use of cliches and timeworn expressions or slogans that have been overused.

14. Enlarge your speaking vocabulary by reading excellent literature and by cultivating a taste for the meaning of words.

15. A study of poetic and prose diction will add color and richness to your own use of words.

2
The Study of Poetic Diction

The person who stands in the pulpit would do well to study poetic diction because poetry is the language of emotion and imagination. A good sermon should appeal to emotion and imagination as well as to reason. Let us look at some rules of poetic diction.

The Rules of Poetic Diction

Poetic diction abbreviates or omits particles. For example, "When day was gone." *The* is omitted. "Not fearing toil nor length of weary days." This form of poetic diction was found in Wordsworth's poetic diction.

Browning omitted the relative pronoun. "You have the sunrise now, joins truth to truth." *That* is omitted. "The hills which he so oft had climbed." "Oft" takes the place of *often*. For the sake of sound and brevity, poetic diction makes free use of abbreviation.

Many Black preachers are masters of poetic diction. They are skilled in word painting and poetic picturesqueness. James Weldon Johnson gives excellent examples of poetic diction in his classic book of Black sermons called *God's Trombones.*

At Bishop College in Dallas, Texas, at the forty-sixth Annual Lacy Kirk Williams Institute for the Ministry and the Laity, Dr. Gardner C. Taylor used poetic picturesqueness in a message entitled "It Is Finished." In his conclusion, Dr. Taylor placed upon the lips of Jesus these words:

"Father, I turn myself over to Thee. The battle is fought and the victory has been won.

"Father, the price has been paid.

"Father, hell has lost.

"Father, God has won.

"Father, evil has shot its last bullet.

"Father, the tide of destruction has been turned back.

"Father, I am coming home.

"Angels, get my mansion ready! I'm coming home!"

Skillful Use of Poetic Diction by Black Preachers

In poetic picturesqueness, the preacher may use an epithet.[1] An epithet is a descriptive adjective. The root or derivation of epithet comes from the Greek *epi* which means from, and *tithemi,* to add. Together, these words mean to give some descriptive or characterizing feature. First of all, there is the essential epithet which expresses some quality in a noun, such as "wet waves" and "green pastures." Secondly, there is the decorative epithet, such as "the beaten work of mountain chains surrounding the holy city." Thirdly, there are phrase epithets, such as this expression from Keats: "So those two brothers, with their murdered man rode past fair Florence." Lamb gives this example: "While childhood, and while dreams, reducing childhood, shall be left, imagination shall not have spread her holy wings totally to fly the earth."

Dr. Emmanuel Scott is known from coast to coast for his unique use of poetic diction. As a Bishop College-trained scholar, no Baptist pulpiteer surpasses his use of alliteration, which is the name given to a near recurrence of the same initial sound. It is a very natural, stylistic device in English. Of the famous English poets, Swinburne made free use of alliterative verse. However, Dr. Scott gives a more contemporary use of alliteration in his sermon book, *The Gospel for the Ghetto.*[2] All through the book numerous examples of alliteration appear on almost every page. An example of alliteration comes from the preaching of the author of this manuscript when he writes: "The preacher points his hearers away from himself to the powerful and profound person of Jesus

Christ." The words beginning with the letter *p* set up the musical structure of alliterative expression.

Sometimes, poetic diction can be overworked in preaching. When this occurs, people forget the message and remember only the decorative speech. When poetic diction is not overdone, the sermon has a quality of beauty.

Contrasting Poetic Diction with Prose Diction

Prose diction is different from poetic diction. It is more popular and is in greater use than poetic diction. Teachers of speech and of preaching counsel students to give greater attention to prose diction than to poetic diction. *Prose* comes from the Latin *prosa.* It is a contracted form of *prorsa,* which is a contraction of the compound *pro-versa,* an adjective feminine in form because the noun to be supplied is the feminine *oratio,* (discourse) the whole meaning, therefore, "straightforward discourse." Prose discourse is straightforward speaking in two ways. First of all, it is not changing the natural order of words; and, secondly, it is not departing from the common use of words. Prose arranges words according to the requirements of directness and emphasis. Poetic diction uses symbolic words. Prose diction uses presentive words. The presentive are those which, by themselves, present a definite conception to the mind, such as nouns, verbs and, to a lesser degree, adjectives and adverbs.

Dr. Benjamin Mays, former president of Morehouse University in Atlanta, Georgia, and a popular Baptist preacher, is noted for his use of prose diction. In a speech given at Interdenominational Theological Center and on the campus of Gammon Theological Seminary, in August 1977, Dr. Mays used beautiful and lucid language. He said:

> Education is designed to train the mind to think clearly, logically and constructively; to train the heart to understand and sympathize with the aspirations, sufferings, and injustices of mankind; and to strengthen the will to act in the interest of the common person. To state the purpose in Christian perspective, the aim of education should be to glorify God and to serve humanity.[3]

Dr. Mays preaches a simple but deep message. He is a paradoxical preacher in that he has the art of saying clearly things of a profound nature. The power of his presentation is clarity. His style is disarming because of the directness of his message. Each of his hearers cannot help but feel the personal nature of the message. The preaching of Dr. Mays has movement so that the audience does not tire of hearing the sermon. When the conclusion of the sermon begins, the audience is sad because this master of prose diction will soon utter the last word of the message.

In concluding a sermon, no one could excel the late Dr. Sandy F. Ray in using prose diction through role playing. In a sermon called "Pilate's Dilemma," Dr. Ray said:

> Pilate, where are you? I saw you swinging on a dilemma. I saw you washing your hands. I heard your public admission that you found no fault in him. But you missed the boat by your failure to commit your life to him. You did not discern that this humble, cross-bound peasant was indeed *The King.*[4]

Dr. Sandy F. Ray was a master of both poetic and prose diction. His sentences were short, crisp, and clear. His verbs were filled with energy. His sentences built up to a climax. When his messages concluded with role playing, before taking his seat, he would always quote the verses of a hymn. The hymn would be related to the sermon and the words of the hymn would add poetic diction. In the sermon "Pilate's Dilemma," Dr. Ray quoted the words of "I Have Decided to Follow Jesus."

Not every preacher can be a Sandy F. Ray or a Robert G. Lee. But each preacher can improve in the use of poetic and prose diction simply by reading the sermons of the great preachers with an ear for discovering the mechanics, tools, and homiletical techniques that they used. After hearing preaching critically, the preacher can then attempt to develop his or her style by using the principles which have made the masters experts in communicating the gospel.

Notes

1. The widely accepted use of epithets belies the Greek origin and uses of the word in a derogatory sense. This is not my use of the term.

2. Emmanuel Scott, *The Gospel for the Ghetto* (Nashville: Broadman Press, 1973).

3. The author copied the words from a speech by Dr. Mays.

4. Sandy F. Ray, *Journeying Through a Jungle* (Nashville: Broadman Press, 1979), p. 130.

3
The Use of Figures of Speech

Skill in the use of prose or poetry requires a knowledge of the proper use of figures of speech. This knowledge utilizes clearness and concreteness in expressing the ideas of the sermon. Some of the most important figures of speech are metaphor, simile, synecdoche, hyperbole, personification, apostrophe, exclamation, interrogation, antithesis, epigram, and climax.

Metaphor

"Jesus is the Lion of the tribe of Judah" is a metaphor. A metaphor uses the verb *is* in painting a word picture and identifies the subject with the predicate in a direct statement. A biblical example of a metaphor is: "The Lord is my shepherd" (Ps. 23:1); whereas a simile uses *like* and *as* in order to make contrasts and comparisons. A biblical example of similes is "he shall feed his flock like a shepherd" (Isa. 40:11).

The Black Christian experience in America has used both metaphor and simile in expressing the heart and soul of faith. From the lyrical utterances of the spirituals came:

> Sometimes, I feel like
> a motherless child,
> Sometimes, I feel like
> a motherless child,
> Sometimes, I feel like
> a motherless child,
> A long ways from home.

or the opposite mood:

> Sometimes I feel like
> an eagle in de air.
> Some a dese mornin's
> bright an' fair
> I'm goin' to lay down
> my heavy load.
> Goin' to spread my
> wings and cleave de air.[1]

Inexperienced speakers sometimes incorrectly use metaphors. They use mixed metaphors. Even Shakespeare used mixed metaphors in saying " . . . to take *arms* against *a sea of troubles.*" Perhaps this was permissible since Hamlet, the user of those words, was contemplating suicide.

Synecdoche

The use of metaphor and simile is often followed by the use of synecdoche. When a part of a thing is taken for the whole, the speaker is using synecdoche. An example is a passage from the Old Testament: "They shall beat their swords into ploughshares, and their spears into pruninghooks" (Isa. 2:4).

Hyperbole

Saying more than is meant is called hyperbole, and it differs from synecdoche. This form of exaggerated language was widely used in the biblical world. In Romans 9:3, Paul used hyperbole: "I could wish that myself were accursed from Christ for my brethren." In Matthew 6:3, Jesus said: "Let not thy left hand know what thy right hand doeth."

Personification

Personification is the addressing of inanimate objects as if they were living. Some examples of personification are: "Doth not wisdom cry? and understanding put forth her voice? She standeth in the top of high places, by the way in the places of paths" (Prov. 8:1-2). "Wisdom hath builded her house, she hath hewn out her seven pillars" (Prov. 9:1).

Apostrophe

Apostrophe is sometimes confused with personification. Apostrophe has a very thin line of difference from personification inasmuch as it addresses the object personified. "O Jerusalem, Jerusalem, which killest the prophets" (Luke 13:34) or "O death, where is thy sting? O grave, where is thy victory?" (1 Cor. 15:55) are examples of apostrophe. The use of the dramatic can be overdone. It is wise for the preacher to refrain from extravagance in the use of figures of speech.

Exclamation

Exclamation is the most spontaneous expression of emotion. It is not the same as interjectional words such as *ah, oh,* or *hush.* Many Black preachers use interjectional words, but they also use exclamation. In using exclamation, the preacher would not say, "We serve a wonderful God." He would say, "What a wonderful God we serve!" In other words, the preacher would use inverted sentence structure.

Interrogation

Interrogation is a figure of speech worthy of investigation. Interrogation asks a question not for the purpose of obtaining information, nor even as an indication of doubt, but in order to emphasize the reverse of what is asked. In Romans 8:31, Paul used interrogation: "What then shall we say to this? If God is for us, who is against us?" (RSV).

Antithesis

Antithesis is a figure of speech which places opposite ideas in juxtaposition. The purpose of antithesis is to emphasize the truth of ideas by contrast. An example of antithesis is Isaiah 1:18: "Come now, let us reason together, saith the Lord: though your sins are like *scarlet,* they shall be as *white as snow;* though they are *red like crimson,* they shall become *like wool*" (RSV, author's italics).

Epigram

Epigram employs in modified form the principle of contrast, or antithesis, in order to give point to a thought. It has come to be popularly accepted as meaning a pungent way of saying things. Epigrammatic sayings must be brief, and they must give some unexpected turn to the idea. They can play on words, such as "The time will come when modern Christians will learn that their ease in Zion is their disease." Or, epigrammatic utterances can express a truism, as was done by Pilate in John 19:22: "Pilate answered, What I have written I have written."

Climax

Climax depends upon the law that a thought must have progress. It is logical in the ordering of thought; this order increases in interest, significance, or intensity. The derivation is from the Greek *klimax*, which means "a ladder." An example of a sentence that uses climax is: "He has showed you, O man, what is good; and what does the Lord require of you, but *to do justice and to love kindness,* and *to walk humbly with your* God" (Mic. 6:8, RSV, author's italics).

Repetition

In examining the written sermons of masters of figures of speech, it was impossible to ignore the late Dr. Robert G. Lee. Without appearing monotonous, Dr. Lee spoke of sin in the following manner displaying repetition:

> Sin is enmity against God. Sin is enmity against God's attributes. Sin is enmity against God's government. God never yet revealed a design which sin hath not withstood. God has never given a command which sin has not trampled under foot. Sin would depose God from His sovereignty—abusing His goodness, abhorring His holiness, vilifying His wisdom, insulting His omniscience, denying His justice and His power.[2]

Dr. Lee expressed the same thought in the first five sentences, but he changed sentence structure and prepositional phrases in a skillful display of the use of repetition. Dr. Lee was a prince among Southern Baptist preachers of his era of oratory.

Contrast

The late Dr. Sandy Ray illustrates the creative use of repetition in emphasizing the word *oasis.* Dr. Ray was a prince among National Baptist preachers of his day. Said Dr. Ray:

> You must not accept the wilderness as your permanent home. You must have a sustained discontent with the jungle. We must enjoy the oasis, but we must not camp there. Saints may shout at an oasis, but the Promised Land still looms before them. The Christian church should always be an oasis in the jungle. It should be a haven for tired, wounded, foot-sore travelers. The most dedicated saints grow tired along this journey. Abraham, Moses, Joshua, Elijah, David, Paul, and even our Lord, grew tired. This is a part of the journey.[3]

Dr. Ray used the term *oasis* three times in succession, contrasting it from the jungle in a dramatic fashion, while painting a different word picture in each of the three sentences. Dr. Ray used repetition with a creative imagination. The listeners were able to identify with each of the mental images.

Elegance

The truly great student of preaching uses elegance of style in the sermon. This is because the preacher selects very carefully the poetry, prose, clarity, energy, and skill necessary in creating mental images germane to the experiences of those in the audience.

Quotations

Quotations are selected from wide reading in history, drama, theater, journals, newspapers, and books. The studious preacher will work very hard to have a sermon filing system that will preserve quotations and reading material according to themes, special days, and authors and sources. Each preacher should be careful to arrange the filing system in such a way that pertinent material will not be buried in the files. Dr. Gardner C. Taylor shared with the author the fact that certain of his members share with him literature and quotations from their reading which could be used in sermons. Dr. Harry Emerson Fosdick had several research people who provided him with material for use in sermon development.

Notes

1. James Weldon Johnson and Rosamond Johnson, *The Book of American Negro Spirituals* (New York: The Viking Press, 1951), pp. 40-41.

2. Paul Gericke, *The Preaching of Robert G. Lee* (Orlando, Florida: Christ for the World Publishers, 1967), p. 104.

3. Sandy F. Ray, *Journeying Through a Jungle* (Nashville: Broadman Press, 1979), p. 28.

4
The Use of the Voice
in Developing Your Preaching Style

The Relationship of the Voice
to Preaching Style

The voice of the preacher determines to a great extent the style of the preacher. The preaching voice, like the musical range of the instruments in an orchestra, has both limitations and possibilities. A person with a soft voice must preach in a conversational style. One who has a deep voice can thunder with the power of a John the Baptist. The human voice can challenge, charm, convince, and comfort. The wise person knows how to use the voice to reach all of these possibilities without straining or placing too much stress upon the vocal mechanism.

The Preaching Voice as a Musical Instrument

Each voice is different because of the differences in vocal structures. Your vocal mechanism is peculiar to you. This is also true of each musical instrument. The violin has a unique quality of tune which is produced by certain kinds of wood that have been fashioned in various ways; thus, every violin has different possibilities for richness of tone. The vibrant tones that are produced depend on the ability of the artist who must know the science and art of mastering the instrument. A good speaker should listen to the soloist or instrumentalist who knows how to improvise and produce a variety of artistic tonal expressions in interpreting a musical score. The voice is the preacher's trumpet for proclaiming the gospel. Each preacher should give the same care and attention to the voice as the trumpet player does in caring for and in tuning his instrument.

The Four Vocal Mechanisms of Preaching

Four mechanisms operate in preaching. The preacher should understand the elementary principles which govern the operation of these mechanisms:

1. *The Motor:* Air expelled from the lungs by thoractic and abdominal muscles furnishes the power for speech.
2. *The Vibrators:* The air stream set into vibration by the vocal folds in the larnyx—the sound-production room—causes phonation.
3. *The Articulators:* The vibrated air stream is then articulated into various sounds by the teeth, lips, and tongue.
4. *The Resonators:* The vibrated air stream is reinforced and amplified by hard substances, as the palate, teeth, bones, and by certain resonating cavities, as the oral, nasal, pharyngeal, and laryngeal cavities.

Proper Breathing

In using the four mechanisms properly, the preacher must learn the proper teachnique for breathing. This controlling of the breath stream is as important for the interpreter of the gospel as it is for the singer, the swimmer, the runner, or the trumpet player. Each has a unique technique. The necessary controls for the preacher are:

1. Learn to use the outgoing air stream so that there is an adequate supply of residual air.
2. Learn to control breathing so that the listener is never conscious of lack of breath or of forced breath.
3. Learn to control breathing so that when you wish to project tones, the power comes from the abdominal muscles.

Your tonal quality may not be as rich as Dr. William A. Jones of Brooklyn or Dr. Kelly Miller Smith's of Nashville, but your nasal resonance can please your listeners. First of all, practice saying nasal continuants—*m, n, ng,*—so that they are properly resonated in the nasal cavity. Another kind of nasality is characterized by "nasalization" of the vowels. Some persons, either because of poor speaking habits or emotional tensions, show an imbalance of nasal resonance on the vowels. You can very easily nasalize the vowels by tensing the jaws, by humping the back of the tongue, or by overtensing the pharyngeal muscles. Some persons prefer to call the nasalization of vowels a "cul-de-sac resonance." This is nasality which should be avoided and not nasal resonance which is acceptable. In addition to the two unacceptable types of nasality just described, there is another undesirable type called "nasal twang." The cause of it seems to originate below the pharynx in the larynx. You can hear this "nasal twang" in some parts of the South, in certain parts of New England, and among persons living under the tension and noise of the city. Some television stars use the nasal twang to portray their characters. Gomer Pyle was such a "hillbilly" Army character who spoke with a "nasal twang." Jazz musicians, such as John Coltrane, used the saxophone to produce the whine or rasp in securing this twang-type resonance.

The quality of your voice is important. Quality is the primary basis of intelligent vocal expression. The preacher with a trained voice can make the gospel interesting, and a well-prepared sermon preached with a cultivated voice can be overpowering. The student minister and seasoned preacher should not only work hard on sermon content but also should work to improve the quality of the voice in pitch, attack, touch, tempo, and inflection. The first essentials for good quality are the mastery of breathing in speaking and the developing of natural vocal skills. Dr. Henry C. Gregory, III, of Washington, D.C., is a preacher who has mastered the conversational style of preaching. Without a great deal of musical variety in his voice, Dr. Gregory, through proper breathing and voice control, uses oratory to move the masses.

Dr. S. M. Lockridge of San Diego, California, has mastered the art of using a natural pitch in speaking. He does not use the preacher's voice, or the holy tone, which characterizes many preachers. Yet, he is in great demand around the world as a preacher. You can develop your voice just as he has done. You may develop your natural pitch by practicing the following five steps:

1. Hum down the musical scale until you reach your lowest comfortable note. That means you can prolong the low note loudly and clearly without any vocal quavers.
2. Now, produce that low tone several times. Call it *do.* Drawl it out as long as your breath supply permits.
3. Begin on that *do* and sing up the musical scale four notes: *do, re, mi, fa.* Prolong the fourth note, *fa.*
4. Begin at your low *do* again and sing up the musical scale five notes: *do, re, mi, fa, sol.* Prolong the fifth note, *sol.*
5. Either *fa* or *sol* is your natural pitch. You will have to decide which of the two is more comfortable after you repeat the exercise many times.

Once you discover your natural pitch, remember that you must use it as the runway from which most of your inflections should start. The main inflections used by the preacher are *upbend, downbend, sweep,* and *slide.* The *upbend* is a slight upward movement of the voice on a syllable. It is used to express questions, indecision, or an incomplete thought. Questions that demand a yes or a no answer take the upbend on the last syllable. The *downbend* is a slight movement downward of the voice. The speaker lowers the voice to express the end of a thought. The *sweep* is more complex. It is composed of a slight upward and downward movement of the voice during continuous speaking. It may occur on one word or be distributed over a phrase. Sweeps express contrasts and comparisons. Sweeps prevent the monotone in speaking. A climactic sweep is a series of stressed words, each one more intensively emphasized than the last. The preacher uses the climactic sweep to express repetition, excitement, and suspense. The vanishing sweep is used to simulate dying out or fading away and to express pity and sorrow. The *slide* is a sustained movement of the voice up or down the gamut. On the uptake, it expresses excitement; on the downgrade, depression. Dr. D. E. King of Chicago,

Illinois, is a master of the slide. Dr. King usually pauses after the slide so that the hearers can feel the emotion and meditate upon the content of the sermon. Seasoned and nationally known Dr. C. A. W. Clark uses a variation of the slide which is the *pitch shift.* This pitch shift reminds the listeners that Dr. Clark is about to enter into the conclusion of his sermon or is moving from one point in his sermon outline to another point. The pitch shift is a form of vocal paragraphing, or a shifting of gears, in oral speech. It is similar to the modulating or changing of keys in a musical score. The pitch shift also allows the vocal chords to rest, and it enables the listeners to relax during the sermon delivery.

Persons like Dr. E. V. Hill of Los Angeles, California, and Dr. R. T. George of Oakland, California, are blessed with good timbre. Dr. Hill makes you listen in awe at his wide vocal range. Preacher-singer R. T. George, as well as Pastor Fleetwood Irving of Vallejo, California, can speak passionately, placing great stress upon their voices; but, upon completing their messages, they can sing with the intensity of professional vocalists, without having damaged their vocal chords. Very few should try to imitate these men. Nature has endowed certain persons with unusual timbre. Timbre is the thing that makes each voice distinctive. It is the result of natural gifts plus experience, training, and creativity. Timbre is the personality of the voice. Your timbre can be cultivated through rigid self-discipline. Hence, you should strive to be the best preacher you can be.

Take good care of your voice. Avoid unnecessary stress. Allergies, head colds, and respiratory infections can affect the quality and functions of your voice. Therefore, the preacher should maintain good health habits. Do not allow anyone to force you to preach in a draft or in a physical setting where you will lose your voice before you can complete your message. Check very carefully the acoustics of the building, and also check the public address system. Demons have been known to invade microphones. A shortage can occur in the microphone at an inopportune time. An usher bringing you ice cold water before you preach can produce harm to the vocal chords. Speaking when one has not had enough fluids to drink, or when one is dehydrated, will impair the vocal presentation of the sacred message. Through experience with your body and its response to the physical environment, you will learn how to care for your voice.

5
Sermon Arrangement and Style

Sentence Structure

The preacher must be a student of sentence structure. The sentence may consist of one word: Sing! Pray! Preach! Witness! Each word just expressed in the imperative mode was a sentence. In preaching, the tendency is to use simple and clear sentences, rather than long, complex sentences with dependent and independent clauses. The main purpose of a sentence is to express a complete thought.

In order to express a complete thought, a sentence needs a subject and a predicate. The subject is the word or word group that tells what or whom the speaker or writer is talking about. The predicate is that part of the sentence that tells what the subject is doing or what happens to the subject. In order to see the relations that exist between words in a sentence, the preacher should make use of a simple chart or diagram.

1. Diagram of subject and predicate:

| The old church building | was sold recently |
| complete subject | complete predicate |

2. Diagram of compound subject and compound predicate:

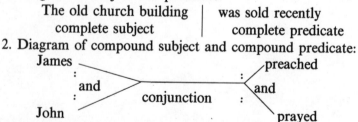

Sentences fall into four groups:

1. The preacher spoke well. (declarative sentence)
2. Did the preacher speak well? (interrogative)

   3. Preacher, speak well! (imperative)

   4. How well the preacher spoke! (exclamatory)

In many sentences, the subject is not acting. Compare:

   1. The facts of conversion were easy for Paul to recall.

   2. It was easy for Paul to recall the facts of his conversion.

   3. Paul found it easy to recall the facts of his conversion.

All three sentences are grammatically correct. The difference is in the stress placed upon Paul.

   1. There are no seats left in the sanctuary.

   2. No seats are left in the sanctuary.

The difference between the two sentences is one of emphasis. The first sentence is more colloquial and less emphatic; the second, less colloquial and more emphatic.

   1. I have only *one* point to make in this sermon.

   2. I have to make one point *only* in this message.

The first sentence stressed the word *one*. The emphasis in the second sentence was *only*.

   1. The service began by singing, "All Hail the Power of Jesus' Name." (awkward sentence structure)

   2. The service began with the singing of "All, Hail The Power of Jesus' Name." (revised sentence structure)

Paragraph Construction

A series of sentences that are coherent and logical make up a paragraph. The purpose of a paragraph is to present a unit of thought. Each paragraph has a topic sentence. The topic sentence is the controlling idea of the paragraph. It may be the first sentence of the paragraph, depending upon whether the writer is using a deductive approach to develop an idea. The deductive approach is the stating of a thesis, or point of view, in a beginning sentence and the sentences which follow explain or expand upon the ideas of the topic sentence.

Dr. Martin Luther King, Jr., was very easy to follow because his oral presentations were logical presentations of topic sentences which he developed with illustrations, quotations, proverbs, and oratory. Seldom did he move to the topic sentence from the method of effect to cause. Although, in the structure of his messages, one could denote his moving inductively from the world of his audience into the biblical world of his text. Dr. King was also a master in the use of transitional sentences.

Transitional Sentences

The transitional sentence concludes a paragraph and provides a bridge which introduces the new thought of the next paragraph. The following words are connectives used in sentence transition: the correlative conjunctions not only/but also, either/or, and neither/nor. *Meanwhile, so then, nevertheless, consequently, furthermore, finally,* and *therefore* frequently begin summary sentences.

Transitions are used in the sermon to indicate time, locale, and mood. Examples of phrases which indicate time include: in the future, when Christ shall come, at the morning of the resurrection, and the next time. Locale may be noted with phrases like: it was at the place of the skull, when those on the ship were at peace, in Jerusalem, and at the Jordan. Tearfully, she looked at Jesus; steaming with anger, Peter cut the man; peace be unto you; and at the mountains of joy stood the victorious indicate mood.

Transitional words fall into the following categories: *qualification:* but, however, except for; *comparison:* likewise, similarly, just as; *contrast:* unlike, instead, on the other hand; *illustration:* for instance, for example; *concession:* of course, no doubt, to be sure, admittedly; and *conclusion:* finally, in summary, the closing word.

The preacher who understands the science of logically putting ideas together in paragraphs and who also knows how to ably use both topic and transitional sentences is ready to creatively develop a sermon. First of all, the preacher needs to select a subject, such as prayer, stewardship, evangelism, missions, love, power, or justice. Secondly, the preacher is ready to develop a title based on the subject or theme which emanated from the biblical text. Studies in biblical exegesis will aid the preacher in being true to the meaning or intentionality of the text. But creativity and imagination will aid the preacher in shaping the sermon.

Sermon Titles

Style in sermon title creation is an art. Here are examples of artistic title creation: *balance:* Christ or Chaos, Community or Confusion, Jot or Tittle, Profit or Loss; *simple sentence:* The Heart Is a Door; Come, You Who Are Weary; Earth Has No Sorrow; God Can Do Anything. But . . . ; *exclamation:* Stand Up! Acts 3:6, Preach! 2 Timothy 4:2, Wait! Psalm 27:14, Run! Isaiah 40:31; *label:* The Prayer of the Righteous, James 5:16; *word play:* Jail House Rock, Acts 16:25-40; Revival of the Unfit, 2 Corinthians 5:17; *rhyme:* Unity in the Community, 1 Corinthians 12:12-27; *question:* My God, Why? Matthew 27:46, How Far Will Your Faith Take You? Psalm 137:4.

In using sermon titles, the preacher should always display good taste. It was said that a preacher was crass and coarse in entitling the parable of the waiting father to say: "Come Home, Baby, Because Daddy Ain't Mad No More!" Nonetheless, there is no hard and fast rule for the correct time to secure an imaginative title in the steps of building a sermon. Some may wait until the sermon is a finished product before discovering an interesting and attractive title. So then, attention should be given to the introduction of the sermon.

Introduction

The introduction of the sermon is like the porch of a house. The purpose of the introduction is to introduce the audience to the body of the sermon with excitement, interest, and curiosity as quickly as possible. A preacher can open the message with a startling quotation or with a penetrating question. The preacher can set the stage for the message by telling a story or by giving a brief and vivid picture of the biblical scene or central character of the text or context. Sometimes the preacher may simply explain the purpose of the message. Variety should be used in the sermon introduction.

Listeners should not be able to successfully predict how the preacher will begin the sermon. The growing student of preaching will observe television, plays, and movies in order to compare the many ways a play or movie is introduced to the audience. Sometimes suspense is built into the introduction or a portion of the final scene is placed into the events of the introduction. The study of plot construction in novels and plays can assist the preacher in developing a plot for biographical or narrative preaching. A quick transition moves the preacher from the introduction into the body of the sermon.

Body

Preaching in the Black tradition places great emphasis upon storytelling. This does not mean that the Black preacher does not use the method of developing three points in the body of the sermon, nor does it mean that some do not major in argument and logic as preaching is taught and practiced in the major seminaries of the nation. The Black preacher develops the body of the sermon according to the contours of the text and in keeping with thematic possibilities and the laws of exegetical control. Nevertheless, a distinctive of the Black preaching tradition is the development of proving, painting, and persuading in the body of the sermon: proving speaks to the mind, painting speaks to the imagination, and persuading speaks to the emotions.

The sermon is addressed to the total person, and it is a call to action or an appeal to commitment on part of the hearers. In the light of this context, the author of the sermon, as a pastor and student of preaching, is developing a preaching style which majors in storytelling. The narrative method of preaching allows for eye contact and for the development of freedom and innovation. In the early years of my ministry, I prepared full manuscripts of sermons. Lyman Beecher lecturer on preaching, Dr. Gene Bartlett of the American Baptist Churches, U.S.A., once asked me, "How do you expect the people to remember your sermon when you can't remember it? You have to read it." I was then reminded of my grandmother, who prayed that the day would come when I would preach without being a slave to my manuscript. That day has come, but Grandmother did not live to see the prayer answered. But, like Abraham, she lived and prayed in faith. However, I do not lament the many years of discipline that came from writing weekly a sermon manuscript. Now, the writing process continues, but the manuscript is not taken into the pulpit.

The sermon body can be memorized without stress and strain on the preacher. Just as the muscles of the body can be trained so that one can jog several miles without tiring or the swimmer can swim with enjoyment several laps every other day, so can the preacher develop the muscles of memory. Here are some tips for memory exercise which I have used:

1.   Memorize some literary gems, humorous events, and quotations. Memorize Scripture.
2.   Select carefully the items to memorize.
3.   Concentrate on the items that are to be memorized.
4.   Memorize the ideas or the concepts in a logical or sequential pattern.
5.   Visualize what you are memorizing.
6.   Rehearse audibly the chief ideas of the sermon.
7.   Don't fret over a memory lapse while in the pulpit, but accept the new and fresh concept given to you while you are speaking.

Remember that preaching a story is much easier to memorize than a sermon that is intricately outlined.

Some styles of storytelling are: *The Success Story,* "David Versus Goliath"; *The Failure Story,* "The Death of Judas"; *The Spiritual Dropout Story,* "Demas"; *The Story of Reversal,* "The Conversion of Saul"; *The Exposure of the Obscure,* The Elder Brother's Sin in the Parable of the Waiting Father ("Parable of the Prodigal Son").

Conclusion

After developing the body of the sermon, using narration, exposition, and argumentation, the next step in the sermon-building process is the development of the conclusion. The conclusion is the tying of all loose ends together and the enshrining of the substance of the message on the hearts of the audience. The conclusion is when the preacher lands the plane at the airport and the audience is ready to leave the church auditorium to do business, just like passengers who have successfully landed in a plane at the airport. Hence, the good preacher, like a good pilot, should never travel past the place of landing. That is dangerous business. It is harmful to both the preacher and the audience. It makes preaching "much ado about nothing."

There are several simple ways to conclude a message. They are:

1. To summarize;
2. To bring a story to its ending, either a satisfying conclusion or an open-ended conclusion, hopefully one of good news and challenge;
3. To end with an arresting sentence or a memorable quote;
4. To end with celebration;
5. To end with introspection;
6. To end with plot resolution of the sermon story;
7. To end with the mood that the message-story is to be continued in the lives of the listeners or continued as a part of next Sunday's sermon series.

The mechanics of style, sentence, and paragraph structure, the introduction, body, and conclusion of the sermon need to be mastered by the preacher. This mastery is of little effect if the preacher is devoid of a theological understanding of preaching. The next chapter will develop not the *how* of preaching but the *what* of preaching. This effort will enable the reader to look at preaching in a theological context.

6
A Theology of Preaching

P. T. Forsyth said that preaching is "the most distinctive institution in Christianity" and that "with its preaching, Christianity stands or falls."[1] Emil Brunner taught that when the Word of God is preached, "in spite of all appearances to the contrary, the most important thing that ever happens upon this earth takes place."[2] Joseph Sittler said, "Preaching is not merely something a preacher does; it is a function of a preacher's whole existence concentrated at the point of declaration and interpretation."[3] Hence, the most respected scholars and theologians on both sides of the Atlantic seem to challenge those of us who preach to take seriously the preaching responsibility.

Your style and mine should be our own. It should be the very best giving of ourselves that we can present to our hearers. The sermons we preach must be authentic and be the result of prayer, preparation, and perspiration. It must be as H. J. M. Nouwen wrote in *Creative Ministry:* "If the preacher does not want to increase the resistance against the Word, but decrease it, he has to be willing to lay himself down and make his own suffering and his own hope available to others so that they too can find their own often difficult way."[4] Our style should reveal both the preparation of our heads and the emotional strings of our hearts if our message is to reach the heads and hearts of our listeners in order to bear spiritual fruit in the lives of those to whom we preach.

Gene Bartlett has quoted Leslie Weatherhead who told how the gospel turned a person around who was in a desperate state. The newfound Christian called together a group of clergy persons in

Britain and said, "You have the greatest news in the world. But you are not getting it across."[5]

Perhaps this handbook on the elements of style in preaching will have at least modest merit, if it assists those of us who preach in getting the message across.

In order to get the message across, the preacher must clearly understand that the message is God's message. This idea is best expressed by Donald G. Millers' words:

> To preach the Gospel . . . is not merely to say words but to effect a deed. To preach is not merely to stand in a pulpit and preach, no matter how eloquently and effectively, not even to set forth a theology, no matter how clearly it is stated nor how worthy the theology. To preach is to become a part of a dynamic event wherein the living, redeeming God reproduces His act of redemption in a living encounter with men (with persons), through the preacher. True preaching is an extension of the incarnation into the contemporary moment, the transfiguring of the Cross and the resurrection from ancient facts of a remote past into living realities of the present. A sermon is an act wherein the crucified, risen Lord personally confronts men, (persons) either to save or to judge them. . . . In a real sermon, then, Christ is the Preacher. The Preacher speaks through the preacher.[6]

According to Karl Barth, preaching takes place in obedience by listening to the will of God. This idea also suggests that Bible study and prayer precede proclamation. Preaching, therefore, is separate and distinctive from lecturing or repeating moral and ethical axioms. Preaching is more than quoting biblical verses as if they were a string of pearls or props to hold up the thesis superstructure of the sermonic argument. Preaching illumines Scripture. An appropriate example comes from the classical preaching of the late and learned Vernon Johns:

> Time works havoc with our most treasured possessions. Beauty turns to ashes beneath its touch. The channels of rivers and the course of history change. Debris piles on the face of queens and kings, and seashells are left stranded on mountain tops. Our health, our wealth, our friends, our ascendancy go whirling away in the

current of the years. When the sands have run sufficiently, they leave Nineveh but a name and the Parthenon a heap of rubbish. . . . "But whoever hears these words of mine," says Jesus, "and doeth them, shall be likened unto a wise man who built his house upon a rock."[7]

In the Black church tradition, the pastor is thought of as the person who feeds the membership with food for the soul.

After this writer has preached acceptably, Deacon Willie Wade of Allen Temple Baptist Church of Oakland, usually says: "Pastor, you were cooking this morning! I heard you!" In using the Deacon Wade analogy as it pertains to style in preaching, you may infer that the preacher is a cook with a sermonic menu of biblical fare. The preacher must know how to serve the biblical meal so that it will nourish the human soul adequately. The sermonic meal must be attractively prepared, tastefully seasoned with the relevancy of culture, and effectively and gracefully served. The sermon is a tragedy when the sermon is all style and delivery minus biblical content. The preacher's training and efforts in the proclamation event must not interfere with the work of God in confronting, redeeming, and saving persons. The preaching event must be an act of grace in which God's presence and power is active as the Living Word in spite of the human limitations of the preacher. Karl Barth is clear in saying:

> This ministry of the Word depends entirely on what God wills to make of it. Therefore it follows that the preacher must be clothed with humility; that, because of his function as a human mouthpiece, he will be discreet and sober; that, since preaching is, by definition, concerned solely with God, it is not possible to preach without praying that the words spoken may become the call of God to men; and moreover, the whole congregation should join in this prayer.[8]

Preaching is not entertainment, nor is it a show for the display of the preacher's learning, wit, or oratorical skill. Preaching, according to the best authorities in theological and biblical studies, is not a professional service for clients who hire a preacher.

Preaching is the activity of God speaking in, to, and for his world through Jesus Christ, the Living Word. Students of historical exegesis should not be disturbed about a seemingly narrow limitation of preaching inasmuch as the Old Testament points forward to Jesus Christ, and the New Testament is not only the cradle which holds Christ but also it speaks of a future or an eschatology with the Christ who is to come. This understanding of preaching requires from the preacher not only careful exegetical and hermeneutical care, and serious discipline in the art of homiletics and oratory, but also the preacher must bathe sermon preparation with an active and alive devotional life. Prayer and preaching cannot be separated. Barth has said of Luther, Calvin, and the great preachers of the past:

> It was not through the brillance of their virtue, their wisdom or their piety that God was able to accomplish His work with them, but through their humility and their boldness in prayer. And God calls us, as single individuals and in community, to take part in such prayer, which is an act both of humility and victory.[9]

There is an urgency and seriousness about the preaching responsibility. The preacher should pay the costly dues required for developing the preaching gifts. Hours should be spent in disciplined study and in wide reading in theological and secular literature. After reading there should be time dedicated to reflection and meditation upon the material read. This exercise calls for digesting and internalizing the material and adapting it to the needs of sermon hearers. This process is a never-ending one. Therefore, the pulpit is no place for the lazy and nonimaginative person. Prayerful study, alert eyes, sensitive ears, and a compassionate heart are ingredients that form the personality of the preacher. The style of the preacher emanates from the personality of the preacher. No preacher has arrived at the point of perfection in the preaching art. The path to perfection is arduous and painful. Even the most able and widely recognized of preachers confess the pain of the Sisyphus-like project of rolling weekly a sermonic stone up the hill of homiletical preparation. Nevertheless, Paul's words to Timothy ring true today: "Neglect not the gift that is in thee, which was given thee by prophecy, with the laying on of hands of the presbytery" (1 Tim. 4:14.)

Early Black preachers, who took seriously the preaching responsibility, worked tirelessly to perfect the preaching gift of storytelling. Their sermons were artistic pieces of style related to sound principles of hermeneutics. C. M. E. Bishop Joseph Johnson, now deceased, illustrated the principles of hermeneutics and their relationship to preaching style in the Black tradition in his book entitled *Proclamation Theology*. Bishop Johnson earned a doctorate in theology from Iliff School of Theology in Denver and a doctoral in New Testament from Vanderbilt University. Said Bishop Johnson:

> Black preaching is by its nature a story-telling process. And Black preachers have mastered the art of breathing life into both the story and the truth that it teaches. He uses his imagination creatively and he places himself as an eyewitness to the story which he narrates and has mastered the art of role playing.[10]

Bishop Johnson also had the highest possible regard for Professor Henry H. Mitchell's two hermeneutical principles which have shaped the style and content of Black preaching. Professor Mitchell said that "one must preach in the language and culture of the hearers" and that "the gospel message must speak to the needs or life situation of the listeners."[11] What has been set forth by Dr. Mitchell as hermeneutical principles which affect the sermon content and style should be the sine qua non for all preachers, irrespective of ethnicity or academic achievement. The purpose of preaching is to communicate clearly the message given to the preacher by God.

Preaching in the idiom of the culture does not mean the lowering of standards in the use of the English language. No one would ever accuse Dr. Gardner C. Taylor of using inelegant language. Yet, no one would ever be guilty of saying that the people of this era did not understand his language. In an October 1983 visit to the Allen Temple Baptist Church of Oakland, California, Dr.

Taylor passionately pleaded with the younger ministers to work harder in perfecting their gifts in preaching. The standard of excellence in preaching must become the standard of each preacher who is aware of the deep intention and vast and varied meaning of the gospel. The cosmic importance of the message is so rich and fertile that the preacher cannot help being claimed by it in reading: "And all things are of God, who hath reconciled us to himself by Jesus Christ, and hath given to us the ministry of reconciliation; To wit, that God was in Christ, reconciling the world unto himself, not imputing their trespasses unto them; and hath committed unto us the word of reconciliation" (2 Cor. 5: 18-19). The preacher must know that divisions and discords abound. Alienation and anguish are everywhere. The human spirit is separated from God and from nature. The human spirit also suffers from inward brokenness.

Therefore, "the word of reconciliation" is a needed and welcome word of good news. The most challenging and stupendous effort that ever has commanded human endeavors is the preaching of the gospel of reconciliation. All dreams of a warless world and all programs for social uplift are far less than the message of a reconciled world in Jesus Christ. Therefore, the responsibility of preaching the gospel is royal business, dignified by the weight of the giver of the Great Commission, and demanding the utmost power of a trained and consecrated personality.

Gardner C. Taylor has told us, "We preach a sweet Gospel." Paul Scherer used Paul's words to tell us, "we have this treasure." Bishop Gerald Kennedy has emphasized, "We speak for God." Sandy Ray has reminded us that we have "melodies in a strange land." Our Bible studies teach us that angels are not allowed to proclaim the old, old story of Jesus and his love. Kings and presidents have not sent us as ambassadors to speak, but the God of our Lord Jesus Christ has touched us, anointed us, inspired us, called us, and sent us to preach.

Preach, preacher! Preach sometimes with the clear and powerful blasts of the trumpet! Preach, preacher! Other times, speak in mellow and comforting tones like the soothing sounds that emanate from a cathedral organ!

We must preach this gospel. We must preach when we are condemned by it and for it and when we are claimed by it and commended for preaching it. We must preach with passion. We must preach with power. We must preach with persuasion.

We must preach as we live between the times of resurrection and consummation. We must preach until this night of godlessness ends and the day dawns when:

> Jesus shall reign wher-e'er the sun
> Does his successive journeys run,
> His kingdom spread from shore to shore,
> Till moons shall wax and wane no more.
>
> To him shall endless pray'r be made,
> And endless praises crown his head;
> His name like sweet perfume shall rise
> With every morning sacrifice.
>
> Let ev'ry creature rise and bring
> His grateful honors to our King.
> Angels descend with songs again,
> And earth repeat the loud Amen.

Notes

1. P. T. Forsyth, *Positive Preaching and the Modern Mind* (Grand Rapids: Wm. B. Eerdmans Publishing Co., 1964), p. 1.

2. Emil Brunner, *Revelation and Reason* (Philadelphia: Westminster Press, 1946), p. 142.

3. Joseph Sittler, *The Anguish of Preaching* (Philadelphia: Fortress Press, 1966), pp. 7-8.

4. Henri J. M. Nouwen, *Creative Ministry* (Garden City, New York: Doubleday and Co., 1971), p. 40.

5. Gene Bartlett, The Authentic Pastor (Valley Forge: Judson Press, 1978), p. 41.

6. Donald G. Miller, *Fire in Thy Mouth* (Grand Rapids: Baker reprint, 1976), p. 17.

7. Charles Emerson Boddie, *God's Bad Boys* (Valley Forge: Judson Press, 1972), p. 74.

8. Karl Barth, *The Preaching of the Gospel,* B. E. Hooke, trans. (Philadelphia: The Westminster Press, 1963), p. 55.

9. Karl Barth, *Prayer and Preaching,* B. E. Hooke, trans. (Naperville, Illinois: SCM Book Club, 1964), p. 23.

10. Joseph Johnson, Jr., *Proclamation Theology* (Shrevesport: Fourth Episcopal District Press, 1977), p. 48.

11. Henry Mitchell, *Black Preaching* (Philadelphia: J. B. Lippincott Co., 1970), p. 29.

Bibliography

Styles of Black Preaching

Abbey, Merrill R. *Communication in Pulpit and Parish.* Philadelphia: The Westminster Press, 1973.*

Bartow, Charles L. *The Preaching Moment.* Nashville: Abingdon Press, 1980.*

Bontemps, Arna. *American Negro Poetry.* New York: Hill and Wang, 1963.*

Clark, Glenn. *God's Voice in the Folklore: Nonsense Rhymes and Great Legends.* Saint Paul: Macalester Park Publishing Co., 1956.*

Cone, James H. *The Spirituals and the Blues: An Interpretation.* New York: The Seabury Press, 1972.*

Gonzalez, Justo L. and Catherine G. Gonzalez. *Liberation Preaching.* Nashville: Abingdon Press, 1980.*

Hicks, H. Beecher, Jr., and E. C. Smith. *Kindling Wood.* Washington, D.C.: Metropolitan Baptist Church, 1981.*

Hoefler, Richard Carl. *And He Told Them a Story.* Lima, Ohio: The C.S.S. Publishing Co., 1979.*

King, Martin Luther, Jr. *Strength to Love.* New York: Harper and Row, 1963.*

Mays, Benjamin. *Disturbed About Man.* Richmond: John Knox Press, 1969.*

Mitchell, Henry. *The Recovery of Preaching.* Harper and Row, 1975.

Neubald, Robert T. *Black Preaching.* Philadelphia: The Geneva Press, 1977.*

Owens, J. Garfield. *All God's Chillun.* Nashville and New York: Abingdon Press, 1971.*

Philpot, William M. *Best Black Sermons.* Valley Forge: Judson Press, 1972.*

Rosenberg, Bruce A. *The Art of the American Folk Preacher.* New York: Oxford University Press, 1970.*

Sangsten, W. E. *The Craft of the Sermon.* Philadelphia: The Westminster Press, 1961.*

Scott, Manuel. *From a Black Brother.* Nashville: Boardman Press,*

Smith, J. Alfred, Sr. *Outstanding Black Sermons.* Valley Forge: Judson Press, 1976.*

Taylor, Gardner C. *How Shall They Preach?* Elgin, Illinois: Progressive Baptist Publishing House, 1981.*

_____. *The Scarlet Thread.* Elgin, Illinois: Progressive Baptist Publishing House, 1981.

Preaching and Story: A Beginning Bibliography

Alter, Robert. *The Art of Biblical Narrative.* New York: Basic Books, Inc., Publishers, 1981.

Bell, Martin. *The Way of the Wolf: The Gospel in New Images.* New York: The Seabury Press, 1961.

Bettelheim, Bruno. *The Uses of Enchantment: The Meaning and Importance of Fairy Tales.* New York: Vintage Books, 1977.

Boyd, Malcolm. *Crisis in Communication: A Christian Examination of the Mass Media.* London: SPCK, 1957.

Buechner, Frederick. *Peculiar Treasures: A Biblical Who's Who.* New York: Harper and Row, 1979.

————————. *Telling the Truth: The Gospel as Tragedy, Comedy, and Fairy Tale.* New York: Harper and Row, 1977.

Calvino, Italo. *Italian Folk Tales.* Translated by George Martin. New York: Pantheon Books, 1980.

Claypool, John R. *The Preaching Event.* Waco: Word Books, 1980.

Craddock, Fred B. *Overhearing the Gospel.* Nashville: Abingdon Press, 1978.

Crossan, John Dominic. *Cliffs of Fall: Paradox and Polyvalance in the Parables of Jesus.* New York: The Seabury Press, 1980.

————————. *In Parables.* New York: Harper and Row, 1973.

————————. *The Dark Interval: Towards a Theology of Story.* Allen, Texas: Argus Communications, 1975.

Crum, Milton, Jr. *Manual on Preaching.* Valley Forge: Judson Press, 1977.

Dart, Archa O. *Tips for Storytellers.* Nashville: Southern Publishing Association, 1966.

Davis, Henry Grady. *Design for Preaching.* Philadelphia: Fortress Press, 1958.

Driver, Tom F. *Patterns of Grace: Human Experiences as Word of God.* New York: Harper and Row, 1977.

Drury, John. *Angels and Dirt.* New York: Macmillan, 1972.

Dunne, John S. *A Search for God in Time and Memory.* New York: Macmillan, 1967, 1969.

Eastman, Arthur M., et al, eds. *The Norton Reader.* 3rd ed. New York: W. W. Norton & Company, 1973, 1969, 1965, pages 1060-1082.

Evans, Robert A. and Thomas D. Parker, eds. *Christian Theology: A Case Study Approach.* New York: Harper and Row, 1976.

Fackre, Gabriel. *The Christian Story: A Narrative Interpretation of Basic Christian Doctrine.* Grand Rapids: William B. Eerdmans Publishing Company, 1978.

Farmer, Herbert H. *The Servant of the Word.* Philadelphia: Fortress Press, 1942.

Frei, Hans W. *The Eclipse of Biblical Narrative.* New Haven: Yale University Press, 1974.

Friedman, Albert B., ed. *The Viking Book of Folk Ballads of the English Speaking World.* New York: The Viking Press, 1956.

Fuller, Reginal H. *Interpreting the Miracles.* Philadelphia: The Westminster Press, 1963.

Granskou, David M. *Preaching on the Parables.* Edmund A. Steimle, ed. Philadelphia: Fortress Press, 1972.

Hildick, Wallace. *Thirteen Types of Narrative.* New York: Clarkson N. Potter, Inc., Publisher, 1970.

Hills, Rust. *Writing in General and the Short Story in Particular.* Boston: Houghton Mifflin Company, 1977.

Johnson, James Weldon. *God's Trombone.* New York: The Viking Press, 1927.

Jones, E. Winston. *Preaching to the Contemporary Mind.* Nashville: Abingdon Press, 1963.

Jones, G. William. *The Innovator.* Nashville: Abingdon Press, 1962, 1964, 1966, 1969.

Keen, Sam. *To a Dancing God.* New York: Harper and Row, 1970.

Kermode, Frank. *The Genesis of Secrecy: On the Interpretation of Narrative.* Cambridge: Harvard University Press, 1979.

Kierkegaard, Sören. *The Parables of Kierkegaard.* Thomas C. Oden, ed. Princeton University Press, 1978.

Knox. Ronald. *A Retreat for Priests.* London: Sheed and Ward, 1946.

_____. *The Occasional Sermons of Ronald A. Knox.* ed. by Philip Caraman. London: Burns & Oates, 1960.

Koestler, Arthur. *Janus.* New York: Random House, 1978.

Kort, Wesley A. *Narrative Elements and Religious Meaning.* Philadelphia: Fortress Press, 1975.

Lowry, Eugene L. *The Homiletical Plot: The Sermon as Narrative Art Form.* Atlanta: John Knox Press, 1980.

Macnab, Francis. *Between Two Lives.* Melbourne: Spectrum Publications, 1979.

McClendon, James William, Jr. *Biography as Theology: How Life Stories Can Remake Today's Theology.* Nashville: Abingdon Press, 1974.

Meredith, Robert C. and John D. Fitzgerald. *Structuring Your Novel.* New York: Barnes & Noble Books, 1972.

Mersand, Joseph, ed. *Great Narrative Essays.* New York: Washington Square Press, Inc., 1968.

Miskotte, Kornelis H. *When the Gods Are Silent.* Translated by John W. Doberstein. New York: Harper and Row, 1967.

Mitchell, Henry. *Black Preaching.* Philadelphia: J. P. Lippincott Company, 1970.

_____. *The Recovery of Preaching.* San Francisco: Harper and Row, 1977.

Mosher, Joseph Albert. *The Exemplum in the Early Religious and Didactic Literature of England.* New York: The Columbia University Press, 1911.

Navone, John. *Towards a Theology of Story.* Slough, England: Saint Paul Publications, 1977.

Nicholson, Marjorie. *The Art of Description.* New York: F. S. Crofts & Co., 1928.

Nouwen, Henri, J.M. *Creative Ministry.* Garden City: Doubleday & Company, Inc., 1971.

O'Brien, William James. *Stories to the Dark: Explorations in Religious Imagination.* New York: Paulist Press, 1977.

Opie, Iona and Peter. *The Classic Fairy Tales.* London: Oxford University Press, 1974.

Otto, Anie Salem. *The Parables of Kahlil Gibran.* Secaucus, N.J.: Citadel Press, 1963.

Owens, Lily, ed. *The Complete Brothers Grimm Fairy Tales.* New York: Avenel Books, 1981.

_____, ed. *The Complete Hans Christian Andersen Fairy Tales.* New York: Avenel Books, 1981.

Parabola: Myth and Quest for Meaning. Vol. II, No. 4, (Nov. 1979).

Paterson, Katherine. *Angels and Other Strangers.* New York: Thomas Y. Crowell, 1979.

Pellowski, Anne. *The World of Storytelling.* New York: R. R. Bowker Company, 1977.

Phifer, Kenneth G. *Tales of Human Frailty and the Gentleness of God.* Atlanta: John Knox Press, 1974.

Rabkin, Eric S. *Narrative Suspense.* Ann Arbor: The University of Michigan Press, 1973.

Randolph, David James. *The Renewal of Preaching.* Philadelphia: Fortress Press, 1969.

Reagan, Charles E. and David Stewart, eds. *The Philosophy of Paul Ricoeur.* Boston: Beacon Press, 1978.

Rice, Charles L. *Interpretation and Imagination: The Preacher and Contemporary Literature.* Philadelphia: Fortress Press, 1970.

Ricoeur, Paul. *Essays on Biblical Interpretation.* Philadelphia: Fortress Press, 1980.

————————, et al. *Hermeneutic of the Idea of Revelation.* Berkeley: The Center for Hermeneutical Studies in Hellenistics and Modern Culture, 1977.

Ritschl, Dietrich and Hugh O. Jones. *"Story" als Rohmaterial der Theologie.* Munich: Chr. Kaiser Verlag, 1976.

Rosenberg, Bruce A. *The Art of the American Folk Preacher.* New York: Oxford University Press, 1970.

Russell, Joseph P. *Sharing Our Biblical Story.* Minneapolis: Winston Press, 1979.

Sanders, James A. *God Has a Story Too.* Philadelphia: Fortress Press, 1979.

Sanford, John A. *The Man Who Wrestled with God.* New York: Paulist Press, 1974, 1981.

Shedlock, Marie L. *The Art of the Story-Teller.* 3rd ed. rev. New York: Dover Publications, Inc., 1951.

Shea, John. *Stories of God: An Unauthorized Biography.* Chicago: The Thomas More Press, 1978.

Smyth, Charles H. E. *The Art of Preaching.* London: SPCK, 1940.

Steimle, Edmund A., Morris J. Niedenthal, and Charles L. Rice, eds. *Preaching the Story.* Philadelphia: Fortress Press, 1980.

TeSelle, Sallie. *Speaking in Parables: A Study in Metaphor and Theology.* Philadelphia: Fortress Press, 1975.

Theology Today. 32:2 (July, 1975).

Uzzell, Thomas H. with Camelia Waite Uzzell. *Narrative Technique: A Practical Course in Literary Psychology.* 3rd ed. New York: Harcourt, Brace and Company, 1923, 1934.

Van Seters, Arthur, et al. *Preaching and Story.* Des Plaines, Ill.: Academy of Homiletics, 1979.

Whitman, Allen. *A Gospel Comes Alive: Meditations on St. John's Gospel Informed by a Theology of Story and Play.* Saint Paul: Macalester Park Publishing Co., 1974.

Wiggins, James B., ed. *Religion as Story.* New York: Harper and Row, 1975.

Wilder, Amos. *Early Christian Rhetoric: The Language of the Gospel.* Cambridge: The Harvard University Press, 1971.

Winquist, Charles E. *Homecoming: Interpretation, Transformation, and Individuation.* Ann Arbor: Scholars Press, 1978.

Young, Robert D. *Religious Imagination: God's Gift to Prophets and Preachers.* Philadelphia: The Westminster Press, 1979.

*indicates books listed in a bibliography for the course outline given in appendix 4.

Appendixes

Appendix 1
Some Contemporary Preaching Styles Worthy of Observation and Study

(*Add to this list your own choices*)

Manuscript

William Herzog,	Berkeley, California
Charles Adams,	Detroit, Michigan
Benjamin Mays,	Atlanta, Georgia
Earl C. Stuckey,	Berkeley, California
Father Jim Goode,	Brooklyn, New York
Tim Winters,	San Diego, California

Extemporaneous

William Lawson,	Houston, Texas
A. L. Patterson,	Houston, Texas
Manuel Scott, Sr.,	Dallas, Texas
Harold Carter,	Baltimore, Maryland
Bishop H. H. Brookins,	Los Angeles, California
George McKinney,	San Diego, California

Expository

C. A. W. Clark,	Dallas, Texas
Lloyd Blue,	Los Angeles, California
James Stewart,	Berkeley, California
Nelson Smith,	Birmingham, Alabama
Otis Moss,	Cleveland, Ohio
E. V. Hill,	Los Angeles, California
Wesley E. Wharton,	Detroit, Michigan
Bennett Smith,	Buffalo, New York

Topical—Textual

Vivian Davis,	Texas
Bennett Smith,	Buffalo, New York
Manuel Scott, Jr.,	Los Angeles, California
Johnny Youngblood,	Brooklyn, New York
S. B. McKinney,	Seattle, Washington
T. Garriott Benjamin,	Indianapolis, Indiana

Memoriter and Textual—Topical

E. K. Bailey,	Dallas, Texas
Charles Booth,	Columbus, Ohio
Otis Moss,	Cleveland, Ohio
Ella Mitchell,	Richmond, Virginia

Oratorical

Gardner C. Taylor,	Brooklyn, New York
Henry C. Gregory, III,	Washington, D.C.
Kelly Miller Smith,	Nashville, Tennessee
O. C. Jones,	Atlanta, Georgia

Exegetical

W. J. Shaw,	Philadelphia, Pennsylvania
Elliott Mason, (Greek Scholar)	Los Angeles, California
David T. Shannon,	Richmond, Virginia
Willie Simmons,	Los Angeles, California
Charlie Sargent,	College Park, Georgia
Sister Addie Walker,	Lafayette, Louisiana

Prophetic

Sid Smith,	Nashville, Tennessee
W. A. Jones,	Brooklyn, New York
Jesse Jackson,	Chicago, Illinois
Thomas Kilgore, Jr.,	Los Angeles, California
Wyatt T. Walker,	Harlem, New York, N.Y.
Joseph Ratliff,	Houston, Texas

Narrative or Storytelling

S. M. Lockridge,	San Diego, California
Henry H. Mitchell,	Richmond, Virginia
Harry Wright,	Brooklyn, New York
Gillette O. James,	Oakland, California
Jessie Davis,	Oakland, California
D. E. King,	Chicago, Illinois
Jasper Williams,	Atlanta, Georgia
Donald Parsons,	Chicago, Illinois
M. L. Price,	Houston, Texas

Philosophical

Fred Sampson,	Detroit, Michigan
W. A. Jones,	Brooklyn, New York
M. C. Williams,	Los Angeles, California
L. Venchal Booth,	Los Angeles, California
Emil Thomas,	Palo Alto, California

Theological

Charles Butler,	Detroit, Michigan
Joseph Ratliff,	Houston, Texas
E. A. Freeman,	Kansas City, Kansas
T. L. Willis,	Los Angeles, California
M. C. Williams,	Los Angeles, California
H. Beecher Hicks, Jr.,	Washington, D.C.

Mystical and Magnetic

M. C. Williams,	Los Angeles, California
Howard Thurman,	San Francisco, California

Lyrical

Charlie Johnson,	Oakland, California
M. J. Williams,	Oakland, California
R. T. George,	Oakland, California
Jasper Williams,	Atlanta, Georgia
Donald Parsons,	Chicago, Illinois
C. A. W. Clark,	Dallas, Texas
L. M. Jones,	Washington, D.C.

Nelson Smith,	Birmingham, Alabama
T. L. Willis,	Los Angeles, California
Fleetwood Irving,	Vallejo, California
Jessie Davis,	Oakland, California

Appendix 2
Guidelines for Interpreting a Text

1. Study the time of writing, the place of writing, the purpose of writing, and the author of the text.

2. Discover the person to whom the text was written! What message does the text have for today? How does the text relate to the Black American experience or to the specific needs of your hearers?

3. Study the grammar and rhetoric of the text? Grammatically diagram or parse the text, discovering the key words, such as verbs, adverbs, or modifying words. What light do modifying words throw upon the text?

4. Pay attention to figures of speech, such as metaphors, similes, and hyperboles.

5. Study allegories of Scripture, such as the story of Jonah or some of the parables of Jesus or sayings of Jesus. For example: "The stone which the builders rejected, the same is become the head of the corner" (Luke 20:17). "A sower went out to sow his seed" (Luke 8:5).

6. Compare the text with the context.

7. Discover the doctrinal, social, political, moral, and ethical implications of the text.

8. When possible, and when you can obtain linguistic assistance, seek the meaning of the text words in the original Old Testament Hebrew or New Testament Greek words of the text.

9. Discover what the text has meant to other interpreters. Use the words of others, but quote them or give them credit for the quotation or interpretation.

10. Illustrate the message of the text by utilizing the resources of general literature, personal experiences, newspapers, drama, television, or even your creative imagination.

11. Don't use the text as a pretext. Be honest to the intentionality of the text.

12. Brood and pray over your text. Let its message simmer in your conscious and unconscious mind before preaching it.

13. When you can, build your outline from the text.

14. *Remember:* your text and theme *must always agree.*

15. Do not preach from a subject such as prayer. Preach from a theme such as unanswered prayer or fervent prayer or intercessory prayer. A subject has to be narrowed down to the limits of what can be properly developed in one sermon. This is why excellent pastor preaching is done in a sermon series. You cannot cross the entire ocean of a subject in one voyage. Hence, you need a theme, or several themes, which constitute a sermon series.

Appendix 3
Criteria for Evaluating a Sermon

I. The Question of Authority: Is It Biblical?
   Is the sermon biblically grounded? Does it deal with one of the major themes or some secondary idea of the Bible? Does the preacher understand the historical and theological meaning of the text or passage? Is the sermon compatible with the spirit, message, and person of Jesus Christ?

II. The Question of Relevance: Does It Speak to the People?
   Does the preacher understand the two levels where people always stand—the permanent and the temporary? Does the biblical truth come alive in the contemporary situation? Does the preacher know his people? Does he speak to their personal and social, spiritual, and ethical needs? Does he care for his people? Is there hostility in the sermon?

III. The Question of Vitality: Does It Have the Power of the Holy Spirit and Personal Experience?
   Can the preacher say, "my gospel?" Is the sermon "truth through personality"? Has the preacher been gripped by his message? Has the Holy Spirit breathed power into it?

IV. The Question of Language: Are the Words Simple, Vivid, Concrete?
   Is the language too abstract, technical, pretty, or spiritual? Does the language have an earthy quality about it? Does it reflect life as we experience it?

V. The Question of Style: Is the Sermon Energetic?
   Is the style too heavy, involved, laborious, and ponderous? Is the style vivid, lively, and pungent? Does the style give a visual quality to the ideas?

VI. The Question of Form: Does It have Structure?
   Is it formless like a jellyfish flopping everywhere, with no sense

of direction? Is it a series of disconnected ideas? Is it like a staircase, with ideas as clear as steps, moving in an ascending order to a climax? Like a mountain with various sides of the truth described? Like a stream with clear indications of bends and new directions?

(Chevis F. Horne)

Appendix 4
A Course Outline for Creativity
in Black Preaching

J. Alfred Smith, Sr.

The following is a course outline for developing creativity in preaching. Appendix 5 is sermons prepared by students who took my course on creativity in preaching at the American Baptist Seminary of the West. Appendix 6 is sermons prepared by some of my students who have been trained in The Allen Temple Ministers' Training Program. Those books listed in a bibliography of this course are marked with an asterisk (*) in the bibliography which precedes the appendixes in this book.

I. *Session 1*
   A. Examination of the Course Outline
   B. Statement of the Objectives of the Course:
      1. To study the imagination, inventiveness, and innovation in the interpretation, content, styles of classical Black preachers;
      2. To help the student develop her or his own latent creativity.
   C. What Is Preaching? Why Do We Preach?
   D. The Uniqueness of Black Preaching, or What Is Black Preaching?
   E. A Study of Gardner C. Taylor and Rodney Romney by Listening to Their Preaching on Sermon Tapes
   F. Professors' Lectures:
      1. "The Recovery of Preaching," Henry Mitchell
      2. "The Homiletical Plot," Eugene L. Lowry
   G. Course Assignment:
      1. A written sermon manuscript on Luke 19:1-10

II. *Session 2*
   A. Hearing Sermons on Luke 19:1-10
   B. A Critique of Each Sermon Heard
III. *Session 3*
   A. The Sound of Sense in Preaching
   B. Preaching and the Imaginations of the Heart
   C. Voice, Breathing, and Articulation in Preaching
   D. Sermon Manuscript on Luke 21:1-5
IV. *Session 4*
   Oral
   1. Presentation of sermon manuscripts
   2. Examination of the Black preaching styles of:
      a. William Holmes Borders
      b. Martin Luther King, Jr.
      c. Benjamin Mays
V. *Session 5*
   A. God's Voice in Folklore, Rhymes, Legends, Poetry, and Novels
   B. Preaching Values in Negro Spirituals and Blues
   C. A Tape of the Reverend Ernestine Reems, Pastor of Center of Hope, Oakland, CA
VI. *Session 6*
   A. The Poetic Descriptiveness of the Late Dr. E. C. Smith
   B. Techniques in Narration, Exposition, and Description
   C. Manuscript on Exodus 3—5
VII. *Session 7*
   A. Oral Presentation of Sermon Manuscripts
   B. Figures of Speech, as Used by Dr. Manuel Scott, Sr., and the Reverend Manuel Scott, Jr. (A careful examination of Manuel Scott, Jr., tapes, and a review of Manuel Scott, Sr. written works.)
VIII. *Session 8*
   A. Reading Good Literature
   B. Reaching and Learning from Novelists
   C. Developing the Imagination
   D. The Imagination of Peter Marshall and Frederick Buechner in the Anglo-American Christian Pulpit
IX. *Session 9*
   A. An Examination of the Creativeness of:

1. Doctor D. E. King
2. The Reverend Otis Moss
3. Ms. Thelma Davidson Adair
4. The Reverend Ellen A. Sandimanie
5. The Reverend Katie G. Cannon
6. The Reverend Doctor Leotis Belk
7. The Reverend Henry C. Gregory, III
8. Dr. Charles Adams

X. *Final Examination*
   A. Present a Tape of One of Your Sermons Preached in a Church Where audience participation Can Be Heard and the Movement of the Sermon and Service Can Be Felt
   B. Written Exam.

Appendix 5
Examples of Written Styles of Preaching by Students at American Baptist Seminary of the West

Christ Asks for a Verdict
(Matt. 21:6-12)
Tobina A. Dalton

(A sermon for Palm Sunday)

If Advent is a time of longing, Christmas a time of celebration, and Epiphany a time of pointing out ways God appears to us, Lent is surely a time of wrestling with goals and life-styles, with ultimates, with our enslavement and our freedom. It is a time for worshiping in the starkness of Maundy Thursday (Tenebrae) and the darkness of Good Friday. The search for God in the midst of darkness and despair is very much a part of the agonizing pilgrimmage of post-modern humanity.

On Palm Sunday, we have mixed feelings. We are deep into the season of Lent. It is the time of the year when we remember the suffering and death of Christ; and, at the same time, we are looking forward to the great festival of Easter and the resurrection of Christ from the dead.

When we read the Palm Sunday story, we rejoice in the fact that Christ rode into the city of Jerusalem among the shouts of "Hosanna!" But we know only too well that this joy was short-lived and that, by coming to Jerusalem, Jesus was signing his own death warrant.

Frankly, I am awed by the triumphal entry. Not because of those frenzied cries of "Hosanna! Save us!" but because Christ entered Jerusalem knowing that death awaited him. Listen to his words to his disciples in Matthew 20. In his own realistic way, he told his disciples: "We go up to Jerusalem; and the Son of man shall be betrayed unto the chief priests and unto the scribes, and they shall condemn him to death, And shall deliver him to the Gentiles to mock, and to scourge, and to crucify" (vv. 18-19). Luke says, "They understood none of these things; this saying was hid from them, and they did not grasp what was said" (v. 34, RSV).

They did not grasp it, I suppose, because they did not want to grasp it. How would you and I have felt if we had left our homes and businesses and gone after a man with an imperious call and with the obvious answer to human life, only to have him say that he was going to Jerusalem to die and leave us alone?

The entrance of Christ into the city certainly took everyone by surprise. When a person or a ruler of importance entered the city, he usually came on an Arabian stallion, with a blare of trumpets, and an honored escort of soldiers. However, Jesus came through the gates in a quiet manner, riding the lowest form of animal. He made his way down the hillside with a crowd following and shouting after him. This has always been called the "triumphal entry."

Matthew says that when Jesus entered Jerusalem, "all the city was stirred, saying: 'Who is this?' " (21: 10). The word "stirred" comes from the same root as the word "earthquake." Jesus' coming in shook the city to its foundations! He came not only to present himself and his claims but also to ask a verdict of the people. What would they do about him? He came wanting an answer from them; and, actually, they went right to the heart of the matter when they asked, "Who is this?"

The Jews were looking for a messiah to come and deliver them. Because the heel of Rome was heavy on their necks, they looked primarily for deliverance from the dictatorship of Rome. Jesus seemed strangely unfitted to lead a political movement. He always refused to use political means; he only called to the human heart and asked the kind of loyalty that is above political loyalty or even interests. Moreover, there were strange rumors that this man thought himself in some way identified with Jehovah—their God! And this was blasphemy, for no man could be like God! Was he mad? Was he a fanatic? Was he a demagogue? He had kept on performing miracles of healing wherever he went, and the fame of this went before him. He never stopped doing that, right up to Thursday of Holy Week.

Who was Jesus? That was the point! If he were mad, you could dismiss him. If he were a fanatic, you could forget him! If he were a self-seeker, you could leave him alone! But where did the majestic calm, that moral majesty, come from that could drive the sellers and buyers from the Temple? And how did that fit with the loving, tender, person who sought the shelter of the home of Mary and Martha and Lazarus each evening? From that same person came terrifying words of prediction about the end of the Holy City itself. All these contrasts seem so strange. "Who [was] this [man]?" If God were in him, how much of God was in him?

A terrible necessity confronted them. They had to decide about Jesus Christ. What did they do on that Palm Sunday two thousand years ago? Some of them went home that afternoon and prepared supper and put their children to bed and soon followed them. Seeing Jesus was just part of a day's excitement. Maybe they talked in the evening light about it all; how foolish he was to even think that he could crack Jerusalem! Maybe they pitied him a little. It troubled them for a few seconds, just as a terrible headline troubles us. Then, they put it behind them.

They were part of the city of Jerusalem and, of that city, Christ was asking a verdict. They simply decided not to be there, to keep out of the way, out of the range of fire. Ah, we can do this so easily! We can do it while we keep on going to church and saying the words of faith and even doing many of its deeds. But, in our hearts, we are running away, running away from the Christ who asks a verdict.

Some people that afternoon puzzled about Jesus' saying. They did not run away, but they could not make up their minds. Oh, yes, they listened to find out where Jesus was going to be or speak the next few days; and, perhaps, they told some of their friends of a wonderful man from Galilee. And, when they had seen and heard him, they would discuss the day and wonder whether what Jesus had said was the truth. So many of us carry on an indeterminate debate inside ourselves, between faith and unbelief, between Christ and ourselves. We ask for a book that will straighten us out; but the only thing that will straighten us out is the decision which we fear to make. Some of the the people in Jerusalem did make a decision and render a verdict. And the verdict? The verdict was no! They knew what Christ was asking of them—a wholehearted loyalty. They counted the cost. It would separate them from the crowd they ran with. It would curtail their activities, raise issues in the family. They knew it was right; but it was costly—too costly to accept. So they made a decision; and, perhaps, they complimented themselves on being able to arrive at a conclusion. But it was a wrong conclusion. They decided against the Christ who asks for a verdict.

Some of them rendered another verdict, and the verdict was yes! They belonged to that withering little company as it dispersed after Jesus' death. They took themselves back to their homes and to their hopelessness. They spent three days of bleak despair; their newfound Light failed them—almost the moment they saw it!

Do you think all will be easy for you because you have accepted Jesus? How many of his followers, right in our own time, have themselves suffered crosses and martyrdoms just because they were his followers? Go easy on your hosannas today unless you are willing to feel the nails and suffer the shame, the thirst, the frustrating loneliness, and the forsakenness. We would have had no Savior if he had not shared fully our lot with us. But these few had put their hands to the plough. They were going through with their commitment. When Christ asked a verdict of them, they gave it. The verdict was yes!

What is this stirring that Christ causes in our hearts? It is a questioning of our motives and of our lives. It is a dissatisfaction with what we are and with what we are doing with our lives. It is an emotion of despair touched with an emotion of hope because we know that, with him, we could be so different from what we are! It is an uneasy spirit that longs for better living. It is the remembrance that we have felt this way before and wanted to do something about it but just never did. It is the horrible, haunting feeling that we shall go on living this half-Christian, half-pagan life. It is the shudder that shakes us when we know that Christ is the Truth, the Way, and the Life; and we live for so much half-truth and so many lies. When we see him lifted up, when we feel his nearing Presence, it doesn't speak comfort to us, but question and uneasiness.

Oh, yes! Jesus comes with a stir! He comes with an earthquake! He rode into the city that day and asked a verdict from the city. He rides right into this city today and asks its verdict too. We have many churches in this city, and many of them are well attended and supported. That doesn't answer his demand for a verdict. Jerusalem could have been the city that carried the banner for him. Cities reflect the soul and moral levels of their people. But cities cannot decide; only groups of people and individuals within these groups can decide. What are we doing with the rich treasure of Christian heritage which is ours? Are we looking back in pride? Are we looking forward in dedication, or is it just sitting there gathering dust? Do we in this church dare face what God may be expecting of us? Suppose he asked of us to be a leaven in Oakland, to be so imbued with his Spirit that wherever we go he can speak through us, work through us, use us? What is he asking of us in this, our town or city, as he rides into it again this day and asks for a verdict?

However, the real city into which Jesus comes today is the city of your soul and mind: that city where there is so much of professed goodness and so much of hidden shame; that city where we receive him with joy and then crucify him with forgetfulness and disobedience. Little did many of those people know that that was judgement day for them. Jesus was only a country preacher come to town, a man of marvels but with no position. What did the religious authorities think? What did the political authorities think? Why was there a terrible pull on their souls? Why the inescapable issue and challenge of Jesus? Why? Why? Why? The reason this objective, outside Christ is so unavoidable is that there is already an organic identity between him and our own souls. John says, "[He was] the true light that enlightens every man" (1:9, RSV). If that is true, Jesus who comes to us from without is the one already familiar to us from within. It is as if, like some clever strategist, he already had his fifth column at work within the city he would take. We are as in a plot. It is as if God created us with an affinity for Christ that we cannot ignore. The Great Outsider is already the Great Insider. It was true then; it is true this Palm Sunday.

Christ wanted to rule Jerusalem—not politically but spiritually. He wanted to rule the hearts of his own people—not by political power but by spiritual power. He wants to rule our cities and our towns—not by a new political party but by the loyalty of this city's people to him.

Do you want Christ to rule? Do you believe that whatever sacrifices he asks of you would be in the interests of such a great common good that it would be worth all its costs? Christ wants to rule you and me. He is not a dictator who will enforce his will on us; but he is the Lord who wants us to accept his will freely because it *is* his will. That's why he asks of us a deep decision, a giving of ourselves to him in as complete a surrender as we know how to make. Why is it that the churches get just so much done but fail to do what they might? (And what they might is certainly done by the churches in El Salvador.)

Because our devotion to Jesus is emotional and sentimental, it does not get down into our muscles and into our imagination and our pocketbooks. But he keeps coming back, riding his gentle donkey into our homes and churches, out on battlefields, and into gambling casinos. He rides into history, not to be examined, but to examine. He is the Examiner! He examines all our behavior: in the state department and in the bedroom; in El Salvador and the Middle East; in South Africa and in our county jails. The murderers and manipulators, the skeptics and cynics, keep trying to be rid of Jesus, to kick him upstairs, to get him out of our way; but he refuses to die! He won't stay down for the full count! He keeps coming back, riding his gentle donkey, asking for a verdict!

I want to finish with a true story about Palm Sunday that I read some time ago.

A cowboy listened carefully to the story of the first Palm Sunday and then he looked up and said, "My Jesus must have had wonderful hands."

"What do you mean?" asked some around him.

"Well," he said, "if Jesus could sit on a colt, on which no one had ever sat, an untried, unbroken animal; if he could soothe it and control it and guide it while people were shrieking hosannas in front of its eyes, throwing down clothes before its feet—man, he must have had wonderful hands!"

Yes, and this coming Friday, we shall be thinking again of those hands; the nailprints of love's uttermost is upon them!

And what he can do for one donkey, he can do for another—meaning you and me!

The challenge of this morning's service I would like to be this: you and I realize that the way forward is perfectly clear, and the guiding hands are available. Individually, in the family, in the home, in the community and in the city, in the nation, in the group of nations—Jesus offers his guidance. He is the Master of life! God calls us this morning to put ourselves into his hands; to commit our way to him; to hold on—whatever happens—to the things that belong to peace!

Today is a new day! He comes over the crest of the hill this morning and looks in our direction! We know who he is! We know it all *too* well! This city within us is "stirred," shaken as by an earthquake! He is as truly here as he was in Jerusalem! Will you do today what he has asked us to do for years? Will you become his disciple, in earnest? Then you will be in his house and in his work, not on Palm Sunday and Easter, but on all the days of your life! No one will need to press you to work or to give or to pray! You will do it because you love him and want to serve him! He comes, asking you for a verdict! Will it be this, or will it be that refusal, or that delay which crucifies him on Friday!

> O God, ride into our lives this day.
> Shake us out of our lethargy.
> Shame us for our faithlessness and show us your salvation.
> Too long we have trusted in our own strength.
> Teach us, anew, the meaning of faith.
> > the meaning of hope,
> > the meaning of love.

Help us to make straight his path,
To make ready his road,
That he may ride in triumph on this particular Palm
Sunday, April 11, 1982,
Right into the middle of our hearts!
Amen. Hallelujah.

Let us sing:
"Mine Eyes Have Seen the Glory of the Coming of the Lord."

The Feast of Christ the King
Robert Lee McCree

Today we celebrate, acknowledge, and praise the fact that Jesus is
Lord and Ruler, God and King of the universe—not just the universe
that we are in but all the universes. He is the King of our world and the
King of our hearts. In the Gospel reading for today, it is quite clear that
Jesus is both the King and Shepherd (Matt. 25:31-46), the One who
watches over and guides the sheep along the right paths and keeps them
in safety. But the choice is left up to us as to whether we wish to follow
what the King wishes: namely, to be kind and charitable to one another
and to love God with our whole hearts and souls. Jesus is also a just and
wise King; we have only to look into the Scriptures to see how wise and
just Jesus really and truly is. We have no fear of enemies or foes for our
refuge is in Christ the King! We need to rely not on earthly kings,
presidents, or rulers, for *our* King reigns over the whole universe!

This Jesus is not a king who merely orders and tells us how to act; but
he, himself, practiced what he preached. He wanted to be like the poor,
so as to help the poor. He loves all because all are in his own image and
likeness. Jesus is a King who wanted to be like his subjects. He took the
form of a man to be a man in all things. This King felt the pain of
rejection. This King heard the sound of birds singing sweetly in the sky
above his regal countenance. This King withstood the bitter sting of

being betrayed by one of his chosen friends. This King touched the lepers and healed them. This King consoled many heartbroken people, with the gentle, calm voice of understanding and—yes—sincerity in sharing their grief. This is the King who changed the water into wine at the wedding feast at Cana, so as to make a simple ceremony complete. But, this King, this wonderful yet humble man, carried a wooden cross and died on that cross for all of us. This King wore not a crown of gold or silver but wore a crown of thorns. This King, who stretched out his hands to bless the multitudes, who healed many by a mere touch, who created and fashioned us in his own image and likeness, was nailed to a wooden cross so that we could live forever with him in his kingdom. It is a great thing, a great and wonderful thing to be loved by a king, but especially the King of all creation! The only thing he asks for is obedience and love in the knowing that we will receive the reward of a place in his everlasting kingdom!

And, so, as we continue with this celebration, let us be reminded that we owe allegiance to Christ Jesus who is King of our hearts. We pay him the glory and praise. We honor and give him the praise that is due, and in confidence we can say:

> Under the shadow of thy throne
> Thy saints have dwelt secure;
> Sufficient is thine arm alone,
> And our defense is sure.

Curiosity Is a Function of Jesus
(Luke 19:1-10)
Robert J. Thomas

As I pondered this passage, I tried to incorporate the first rule of homiletics which is to upset the equilibrium. Well, to really upset the equilibrium, the narrator has to upset himself. So, I wracked my brain all week thinking about an appropriate title. I thought: *how about "A Change of Heart?" No! Too simple; everybody expects sermons that speak about conversion. Well, how about "Face to Face at the Ol' Plain Tree"? Nope! Too complex; you'll never remember that a sycamore tree in Judea is equivalent to what is known as a p-l-a-i-n tree in America. Oh! I've got the perfect proverb: "Curiosity killed the cat!" Nope! Too humorous. I don't think the congregation is ready for the cotton patch version of how this cat from the Internal Revenue, named Zach, climbed a pecan tree to check out the "Main Man, Jesus"!*

Seriously, I wanted a title that would stick with you even if you forget every word following the mention of it. So, the Lord woke me up last Sunday morning and gave me, "Curiosity Is a Function of Jesus," or, if you are a student of mathematics: $C = f(J)$!

Since the Passover Days of his youth, Jesus had been curious about God, asking the teachers in the synagogue the meaning of the Old Testament Scriptures. Here, we find a man, Zacchaeus, who sought not only the teaching of Jesus but the Savior himself. Deep down within the bowels of his bearing, Zacchaeus used the known and unknown information of Jesus as a stepping-stone for action. I'd like to use the analogy of skin as a steeping-stone to illustrate the range of Jesus' power.

Skin, defined, is the largest organ of the body. Skin is made up of two layers: the outer one (called the epidermis, or cuticle), and the inner one (called the dermis, or the true skin). Similarly, we have clearly the case of: (1) the OUTER Zacchaeus; (2) the INNER Zacchaeus; and (3) the INTER Zacchaeus.

The OUTER Zacchaeus

Zacchaeus was a tax collector for the Romans who occupied the country; and he was, so to speak, working for the enemy. During this historical period, tax collectors prostituted themselves by buying the privilege of gathering taxes. As a result of his large bribe, Zacchaeus's position read: Chief Tax Collector, or Superintendent of Taxes and President of the Jericho Board of Finance. Head Honcho. Big Fish. V.I.P. (AKA, Very Incredulous Person). And the more he collected, the more he gained. He operated under the same law we coexist under today: those who know the law use the loopholes to extort more benefit and power.

But it's too easy to say years of extortion gave Zacchaeus a guilty conscience that manifested neurotic, unpredictable states of behavior within himself. It's too easy to say Zacchaeus's curiosity was this act of neurosis that sent him climbing a tree to see when Jesus would be coming. Aren't we like the poor, self-righteous followers on their way to the Passover festivities when we stab people in the back, with our eyes, as they climb the economic or spiritual tree of life? For Zacchaeus was not only treated as a social outcast but a moral outcast as well because he had literally "sold his soul to the devil."

But, somehow, somewhere, with regard to the Jewish tradition from which he was raised, Zacchaeus realized that his skin was becoming callous. No one could penetrate it, except possibly Jesus. So, he was curious and sought to know who Jesus really was. Zacchaeus pondered, *How tall is Jesus? Is he a man of normal stature, or short like myself? Brown-skinned like most Semitic Jews, or high-yellow like the Pharisees? Do his eyes sparkle and pierce the inner being of those he meets? Does his voice calm the listener's ear or repel the receiver of his words down the way?* Ah! But Zacchaeus desired to know more than just the periphery. He was curious about the heart of the matter: *Who is this man passing by, who sticks with the blind and the lame and never is too grown up for a child; who eats with the tax collectors and the sinners and is a companion of outcasts, meeting every one without pride or contempt or a feeling of superiority?* Yes! Believe it or not, this was the curiosity that made the Chief Tax Collector forget about his position and title, his wealth and fame, his scruples and exploits.

The INNER Zacchaeus

The INNER Zacchaeus overlooked all the above and became totally captivated in his quest to know who Jesus really was. As Jesus passed, he noticed a conspicuous individual in a sycamore tree with its large patches of flaking bark and dense maple-like foliage, almost barren of fruit, mature branches hung, badly in need of pruning. At the end of one of these branches was a man, hunched and coiled like a snake waiting for the next victim to exploit. And Jesus commanded Zacchaeus, "Come down!"

> "Come down, off your limb of security!
> Come down, off your pedestal of riches!
> Come down, off your branch of deception!"

"Come down, Zacchaeus, as quickly as you can. For tonight I am to be a guest in your house." Zacchaeus carefully unraveled himself to the ground, shocked and amazed at such an invitation. But he obeyed without hesitation.

When Zacchaeus looked into Jesus' face, the dam broke. All of the anguish in his life poured out. And when the crowd saw Jesus receive Zacchaeus openly, they all murmured, saying, "What gall! What audacity! What stupidity! Jesus has to be a guest with a sinner!" There was gossip among the pious and religious for they could not understand Jesus' behavior. Of course not. Jesus always inverts the perspective that we would normally take. He always did and does the unpredictable. That's what is so beautiful about the Christian spirit. No matter how much you plan ahead, trying to be organized, Jesus steps in and allows his plans to be manifested instead of ours.

But Jesus was not just interested in Zacchaeus' physical house. At the moment of invitation, Jesus entered the inner house of Zacchaeus's soul. At that moment, Zacchaeus had a change of heart, a conversion experience, a desire to testify: "Believe me, Lord! I'm turning over half of everything I have to the poor; and if I have squeezed anyone 'between a rock and a hard spot,' I will replace it four times over!"

At first it could almost appear Zacchaeus was just uttering pious moral platitudes, or even that he wanted to brag a little: "Isn't that right, Jesus? Isn't it proper to tithe 10 percent of one's income? But, look, *I'm* giving 50! And if I have swindled anyone, then I'll do 400 percent worth of penance!"

However, one does not have to be a psychology major to understand that Zacchaeus did none of these things for his own prestige. He simply wanted to confess. He realized he had come to a dead end, the end of life's rope, and it was about time to tie a knot and hang on with Jesus.

The closer Zacchaeus came to Jesus, the more his real self awoke in him, the more his outlook was changed and his values were altered. Money became nothing to him. All in a flash he saw something which put his wealth into its proper perspective. He came to see his extortion for what it was—a sin against God and man; a denial of human brotherhood and an outrage on God's children. All these things began to pass through his mind as Jesus and he sat talking together.

The INTER Zacchaeus

Finally, after Jesus penetrated the outer shell of Zacchaeus and got under his skin, it was up to the INTER Zacchaeus to allow the miracle of the gospel to change his life. I would ponder what Zacchaeus probably put on his front door: "I've Got It!" instead of the evangelical bumper sticker, "I Found It!"; for he rejoiced that *now* he knew who Jesus really was. Now, his future had begun. The passage reads: "Today, salvation has come to this house" (Luke 19:9, RSV). Whenever contact with Jesus Christ occurs, there salvation will be also.

With a changed heart and a new relationship with Jesus, curiosity did kill this cat, for Zacchaeus died to sin and opened his eyes to a new vision of God that gave him new life. But not just a new vision—a recovery of the deep, deep truth of the vision of God in Jesus he had lost amid the exploits of life. I am reminded of 1 Peter 2:9 which reads, "But ye are a chosen generation, a royal priesthood, an holy nation, a peculiar people, that ye should shew forth the praises of him who hath called you out of darkness into his marvelous light."

Yes, once God has brought us into the light, there is no way we can avoid reflecting and reradiating the light rays from eternity that have struck us. When Jesus steps into your life, he starts a chain reaction that goes on and on and on, never ceasing, always abounding. The same force that overturned our lives and set us on a new course will not let us rest until we have passed on the message of the good news of Jesus Christ. "For the will of God will not lead us where the grace of God cannot keep us."

When you meet Jesus face-to-face, you are never the same again. Once a believer, always a believer, no matter how much we stray. For Jesus is the Great Transformer, who continues to show the way. He gives us the brightness of the morning as the day begins and peace of mind at its end.

He gives us joy in life and companionship in distress. And when we stand in final judgment, he will intercede for us because he has already paid the price. The Man from Galilee stands between me and every shadow, for he has brought me down from my airy spectator's seat in the trees; and now there is nothing else in the world that can come between me and the final fulfillment of my life.

The Gift of the Two Mites
(Luke 21:1-4)
Roland S. Ruffin

Our passage introduces us to a woman in the court of women at the Temple. She gave an offering for the maintenance of the Temple. It just so happened on the same day that our Lord and Savior Jesus Christ was there also, observing the placement, posture, and position of all who engaged in giving. He saw those who possessed much giving little. There were those who gave much for the maintenance of the Temple, yet so little for the maintenance of their souls. However, the record recorded that there was one who gave an offering, though little in size, yet was so great until it demanded the attention of both the divinity and dust of the Master. For, within the midst of the masses stood a woman who gave two mites.

The record introduces this woman as a widow, not a mother or ordinary woman, but a widow. She was a victim of powers beyond her control, powers beyond her ability to reason or understand; she was a widow. She was one of the unfortunate few whose lives would forever testify upon the written pages of history of the cruelty of death and the ashes of its remains. Death is known for its cruelty, for it takes the warm and replaces it with the cold. It takes the dream of both wife and husband and replaces it with memories. It defeats probability by denying possibility; and, in our passage, death reduced the former glory of a wedding and a wife to the shadow of a widow and two mites. She was a widow, a woman whose position, pride, and identity in Jewish society was robbed by death. She was a widow, a poor widow, for all she could now offer were memories and the tragedy of a bent and broken life. Yet, this marred and mangled shadow of a woman made her way to the Temple and gave a small offering that was so great until silence left its place of above and went beyond the mind to the mouth of the Master. She gave without the utterance of a single word, for what has a shadow to say? But when she gave, silence began to speak and proclaimed its truth. When she gave, faith gave its testimony. When she gave, hope proclaimed its victory over despair. When she gave, silence told the world about love.

Others only beheld an offering of two mites; but within the mind of the Master, it was already known that the mites might have never been given had it not been for truth, faith, and love.

When she gave, the widow became a woman; and the shackled shadow of her outer life fell to the celestial sainthood of her inner heart.

Perhaps we, too, like the widow, have experienced the cruelty of death. Maybe death has yet to take the life of a loved one or dearest friend; but, then, death has other ways of making its presence known for the cruelty of death can be seen in the wages of sin and in the tragic lives of those who deny the gift of God. The cruelty of death can be seen in the lives of those who walk with bones in place and with flesh covering the bones and yet possess no life.

The handiwork of the widow's hands testified of the love, truth, and faith within her life—so much so that the Master spoke well of her. We, too, like the widow, should give our all; for, if we give unto God our all, then, perhaps the Master will speak again as he did for the widow. But, this time, saying, "Well done, thou good and faithful servant. [Enter now into the eternal joys of heaven]" (Matt. 25:21).

The Danger in Listening to the Devil
(Luke 22:1-7)
Albert C. Coleman

During the course of human existence, man has had to listen to many voices. There was the voice of the nurse who said, "It's a boy!" There was the voice of the mother, "Johnny, hush! I'm going to feed you in thirty minutes. I must keep you on a schedule!" There was the voice of the father, "Johnny, choose your friends wisely!" There was the voice of the teacher, "Johnny, you can do much better than average work!" There was the voice of the principal, "Johnny, be the best at whatever career you choose!" There was the voice of the preacher, "Johnny, God made man *equal*—man made up the system of quasi-equality!"

And, yes, there were the voices of the other fold. Perhaps the neighborhood bully said, "Johnny! Try this—fresh from Columbia." Perhaps a well-known piece of femininity called out from a fourth-floor apartment window, "Johnny, we have a sale on . . . twenty-five dollars a ride!" (Her father owned a country stable.) Perhaps the unemployed owner of a Seville offered him a job making money that the IRS could only estimate. Perhaps he heard the voice of a partying student, "Johnny! Slide your test paper over just a little bit more." Perhaps he heard the voice of a high school dropout, "Johnny, why fill your brains with knowledge when you'll never use it?"

The Danger in Listening to the Devil

Yes, my friends, in the course of our lives, we have listened to many different voices. These voices in many ways have shaped our personalities, our attitudes, our dispositions. We are influenced by the people we come in contact with. If we are among people who smile, then chances are good we will smile. If we are among people who fuss, then chances are good we will fuss. If we are among people whose hopes and dreams climax on Friday and Saturday night, then our hopes will point in that direction. If we run with people with a negative outlook on life, then chances are good that our outlook will also be negative.

I thank God that my father ran with people whose outlook was positive. He was a sugar cane worker, a plantation dweller, in Louisiana. With help from above, he was able to motivate six of seven children into completing high school. Four of the six completed college, and three went on to work on higher degrees.

Turning our attention to the Scripture, we see that Satan is spoken of quite often. Matthew 16:23, "Get thee behind me, Satan"; Luke 10:18, "I saw Satan fall like lightning" (RSV). Luke 22:3, "Then entered Satan into Judas." Second Thessalonians 2:9, "After the working of Satan." These Scriptures speak of the presence of Satan. Rookie Bible scholars have had the tendency to call him a "concept." They say, in so many words, that Satan was a part of the *theology of Jesus Christ.* These scholars write books putting forth new ideologies. These new ways of looking at things have confused the mind of the masses. In their mind, sin is a misdemeanor. Victims from this school of thought have watered down the consequences of sin and made it a household word. As we look at society today, we see that man flirts with these misdemeanors on a daily basis.

Alcoholism is on the increase. Its victims can't see the number of graves and broken homes that are caused by the overconsumption of this liquid. They can't see the end result of a light-headed feeling, incoherent thoughts, glassy eyes, and the mental phrase, "Fix me another one." To those who are able to hear, alcohol is a bandit who robs a family of its financial means for a loving existence. Money for a child's education is spent on a case. Money earmarked for the purchase of flowers is used to purchase a gallon. Money set aside for some other worthy cause is quarantined for a quart.

Smoking: the white death of burning dried leaves. This menace to society continues to exist in spite of the surgeon general's warning: "Caution: Cigarette smoking can be hazardous to your health." Can you hear the larynx of the little ones? They are crying out: "In the name of love, give it up!" Do you hear the lungs of the youth? They are yelling, "Why me? Why me? Why me?" Listen to the screams of the arteries and heart! They are screaming for longevity. These screams are a result of the writings of those scholars. They have confused the path of humanity. They write books with strange sounding titles: *Is God Dead, Jesus: Man or Myth, The Death of God,* and so forth. These writings have, in many ways, taken our eyes out of the Bible (the Word of God) and have focused them on books (the works of people). This focusing has led to a dramatic increase in the U.S. cultic movements: The cult of disco; The cult of drugs; the cult of obesity; the cult of over-sleeping; the cult of good-timing; the cult of getting stoned.

Present-day readers of these books can come to only one conclusion: "You only go around once in life—so, let it rip!" Adults who once subscribed to this philosophy could tell you the sad story that in many ways has been captured in secular songs: "Pain in My Heart"; "Lonely Days and Lonely Nights"; "Cry a Thousand Tears"; "Come Back Home, Daddy"; "Just One More Chance"; "Cried All Night Long."

In our Scripture, we find Satan entering Judas. Judas was one of the twelve disciples; he attended meetings with the other disciples. Judas did not agree with all that happened to Jesus. He became angry when the lady used some expensive oil to anoint Jesus as he was on his way to Jerusalem. This tells me that Judas had a liking for money. Money! Money! Money has been at the root of many divorces in the United States. Now, because of this large number, I must ask several questions: Did the marriage take place because of the love of money? Was it because of biological features: big eyes? huge hips? Was it because of force? My friends, let me tell you this day: if a marriage isn't built on the love of Christ, then that's a marriage subjected to the storms of gossip, rains of jealousy, and the winds of insecurities.

Continuing with our story, we see that Judas listened to the devil. The Feast of Unleavened Bread drew near. The rulers of that time drew up secret plans to get rid of Jesus. He went around (if I could use some present-day examples) telling people that it wasn't normal to live with rats and roaches. It wasn't right to be forced into riding in the back of buses. It wasn't just to sentence some severely and others less severely for the same crime. He told them that there wasn't anything wrong with going to bed on a full stomach. Judas was the key to their secret plans. His eyes were filled with dollar signs. Yes! For thirty pieces of silver, Judas betrayed our Savior. He turned good over to bad. He allowed wrong to arrest right. He permitted his enlightened thoughts to be over-shadowed by unenlightened ones. Judas made the error of his life. For what? Money!

Nowadays people do strange things with money: some men put money in a machine, "wishing" that more money would be returned in a pre-engineered slot. Some women undress to perform all sorts of acts in hope of being compensated. (How can a few "Georges," several "Lincolns," and a few "Hamiltons" compensate one for their most personal pride? How?) Children put their lunch money in game machines to sink a ship, pilot a plane, drive a chopper, steer a dragster, make the big kill, or hang from a glider. Nations spend billions on destructive equipment, while the poor and elderly go neglected. Churches spend thousands on travel plans—driving to Louisiana, Texas, or Arkansas—while their scholar-ship funds stagger from oversightedness.

Yes, Judas fell into the trap of listening to the devil. He was influenced by the forces of negativism. He succumbed to the peer pressure of "the little hope" crowd. Judas was immature, unable to think for himself. Judas was a basket case.

Today, you need not listen to the devil. You need not be blown by every wind or doctrine. You need not fall victim of jealousy. You need not be troubled by the storms of gossip.

Jesus paid the price for the sins of the world. He was wounded for our transgressions, bruised for our iniquities, and by his stripes we are healed. Jesus is the Way, the Truth, and the Light! No one comes to the Father except through the Son. Jesus washes away *all* our sins! Come, let him teach you about those voices of evil!

Whosoever will, let 'em come. Let 'em come!

Amen.

A Question for You, Jesus!
(Luke 21:1-4)
Ron Martin Dent

I have a question for you today, Jesus. I have a question I've been meaning to ask for a long, long time. I have a question for you, and it's burning deep inside me. I have a question for you, Jesus, for I see you there, talking in the Temple, surrounded by all the people: the crafty scribes; the pious Pharisees; the wealthy in their long, silk robes and fat, bulging purses; the powerful with their crowns; and the mighty with their slaves attending to their every need. I see you there, talking in the Temple courtyard with its dazzling white walls of gleaming marble and precious stones, bronze doors, golden columns, and silver vessels. I see you there, in the midst of magnificence, watching a poor, destitute widow put her last, meager, pitiful pittance in the offering plate.

Yes, I see you there, Jesus, and I have a question for you: WHY? Why didn't you help her? Why didn't you change things so she wouldn't need to be poor anymore? Why, Jesus, why? After all, you changed water into wine and walked on water. You healed the sick, gave sight to the blind, and made the lame to walk. You had the power to raise even the dead! Why couldn't you spare just a little of that power to do more for this poor woman? Had you forgotten so soon your own mother, Mary? She, too, was a widow, struggling and sacrificing to raise you and your brothers and sisters. Wouldn't her memory move you to do more for that widow than make her an example for countless numbers of Sunday sermons on proper church giving? Why, Jesus, why?

I ask you this, Jesus, because I've seen that widow come into my church, carrying her life's possessions in a clear plastic shopping bag. I've seen her come into my church, looking for a handout, and finding none. I've seen her leave my church empty-handed, yet stopping on the way out the door to put fifty cents in our collection plate for the hungry and needy in our neighborhood. I've seen that widow, Lord. I've seen her come in looking for a handout and leaving empty-handed—and I've felt powerless to help her. Oh, I could have given her a few dollars, perhaps, but I couldn't change the economic system which may have made her poor. I couldn't change her life, to remove whatever misfortune had happened to her. But you, Lord, you had the power, didn't you? Didn't you?

I saw that widow leave empty-handed. But, you know, Jesus, I saw something else. She left empty-handed, but her heart was overflowing! Yes, her heart was overflowing with the joy of knowing that even if no one else could help her, she could at least help someone else. Her heart was overflowing, Lord! And I think that maybe—just maybe—you saw that too. And, you know, Jesus, I think I see why you didn't change things. Why, you already *had* changed things! You were there!

> Where restless crowds are thronging along the city ways,
> Where pride and greed and turmoil consume the fevered days,
> Where vain ambitions banish all thoughts of praise and prayer,
> The people's spirits waver: but You, O Christ, are there.
> In scenes of want and sorrow, and haunts of flagrant wrong,
> In homes where kindness falters and strife and fear are Strong,
> In busy streets of barter, in lonely thoroughfare,
> The people's spirits languish: but You, O Christ, are There.[1]

You are there, Jesus, as you were among the rich and mighty, dressed in your poor, simple carpenter's clothes, to convict us of *our* greed and selfishness. You are there, to invite us to open our hearts to you. And that's what you weren't talking about there in the Temple, wasn't it? You weren't talking about giving at all but about changing our hearts! You didn't help the widow because it really wouldn't have changed things all that much, would it? I mean, Jesus, if our hearts don't change, it's not really a change; is it?

Were you remembering way, way, back then when Pharaoh hardened his heart and wouldn't let your people go? You forced him to change that time, Lord; but after the Israelites left, he hardened his heart right back and led his chariots into the sea to get the Hebrews back. No, if change is not in our hearts, it's no change, no change at all.

But you *are* there, O Christ, and because you are there, you give us the freedom to change our hearts to reach out to others in need. You have given us the gift of dignity given each of us as children of God. You were there, Lord, with the widow as she, with dignity, put her coins in the plate. You were also there, Jesus, at the shelter for homeless men where I worked and saw the dignity of these men maintaining a measure of pride by freely offering part of their monthly welfare check in thanksgiving for a warm place to stay at night.

You are there, Jesus, and you have given us the gift of dignity, and we feel it in our hearts also. But you know, Lord, we don't always open our hearts to change, to choose, and to reach out to others. And maybe that's why you've given us the most precious gift of all—yourself. For you are there, O Christ, when our spirits waver; and, then we see you, God Almighty, clothed not in the power and glory from on high but in the dirty, ragged garments of the poor and needy. We see you, Jesus, among us—sharing in our struggles, knowing our needs, and suffering with us in our pain. You are there, Jesus, hanging on the cross, crucified for us—FOR US! So we may no longer be burdened by the hardness of our hearts. FOR US! So we can be freed from our sin. FOR US! So we, too, can freely give our hearts to you! All that we have—ourselves, our time, and our possessions—are yours, Jesus. You are here, with us and for us! And, so, we ask you, Jesus, from the bottom of our hearts:

> Take my life and let it be
> Consecrated, Lord, to thee;
> . . . .
> Take my moments and my days,
> Let them flow in ceaseless praise.
> . . . .
>
> Take my will and make it thine,
> It shall be no longer mine;
> Take my heart, it is thine own,
> It shall be thy royal throne.
>
> Take my love, my Lord, I pour
> At thy feet its treasure store;
> Take myself, and I will be
> Ever, only, all for thee.

Notes

1. "Where Restless Crowds Are Thronging," by Thomas C. Clark, *Lutheran Book of Worship.* Minneapolis: Augsburg Publishing House, & Philadelphia: Board of Publications —Lutheran Church in America, 1978.

She Hath Done What She Couldn't
(Mark 12:38-44;1 Kings 17:8-16)
David Bunje

The Scripture lesson this morning ended with Jesus calling his disciples and saying, "This poor widow has put in more than all those who are contributing to the treasury. For they all contributed out of their abundance; but she, out of her poverty, has put in everything she had, her whole living" (Mark 12:43-44).

This Scripture sounds like a command to pretty much give everything away. But, we don't! This Scripture appears to exalt the poor. Which we aren't!

Are we Christian?

It is shameful, Jesus said, to dress well and have salutations downtown; yet, we do. Good seats at the show and long prayers at the meetings are condemned, but we *will* have them. If nothing else, this Scripture lesson seems like a great setup for guilt.

Is that what it means to be a Christian: guilt?

You know, widows are a powerful symbol in the Bible. In a society which discouraged remarriage and didn't protect many rights of women, widows were understood as among the least fortunate, most vulnerable members of the community. Many of the Old Testament chroniclers measured the righteousness of their kings by how the widows fared under their reign. The prophet Isaiah railed against those who "turn aside the needy from justice, / and . . . rob the poor of my people of their right,/that *widows* may be their spoil, / and . . . the fatherless their prey" (Isa. 10:2 RSV, author's italics). So when Jesus accused the scribes of devouring widow's houses, in other words appropriating their property and livelihood for the scribes' own unsated appetites, he was leveling one of the most serious charges he could.

In contrast, by using the widow as an illustration of selfless sacrifice in the very next passage, Jesus once again turned the tables, gaining shock value from having the least expected sources for the highest inspiration. A widow, of all people, the most insecure, most forsaken, vulnerable member of the community, is, in this instance, the most laudable.

Hmmmm. What's Jesus trying to tell us?

As readers of this passage, we probably find ourselves identifying more with the scribes than the widows. We easily recognize ourselves as those

who give: to the church, to our families, to our community. We are those
who give out of our *abundance*, still holding the necessities back. You
know, the necessities of money for food, clothing, and shelter; the necessities of psychological stamina in a dog-eat-dog world; the necessities of
control over the destinies of our own lives. Yes, it is difficult to get into
the shoes of the widow, for we are well-off, protective, and calculating
in our giving.

It's nothing new. Back in the fourth century, when Christianity was
first legalized in the Roman Empire and the clergy were relieved of
citizenship burdens, such as military duty and taxation, many of the
wealthy Romans suddenly heard the call to ministry in the new church!
Constantine had to make a law in AD 320 prohibiting the wealthy from
going into the ministry. "The rich should bear the burdens of the world,"
he said. "The poor should lead the church." Those Romans were setting
a fine precedent for folk who use the. church for their own purposes.

Yes, it is difficult to get into the shoes of the widow!

It is critical to note that this Gospel lesson takes place during the last
week of Jesus' life. He had triumphantly entered Jerusalem and was
facing the ultimate expression of his own ministry. Jesus knew he would
be making a sacrifice, like the widow, from his whole life, and he wanted
to communicate what that means. It was what he had to do for his own
sake but also for ours.

This very kind of sacrifice is illustrated by the companion Old Testament Scripture. Again, it involves a widow—the least able, the least-
thought-of—to make the most profound of statements. In a time of need,
Elijah went to a widow for sustenance. What he found was a woman
facing her last supper. All she had was a *handful* of meal and a little oil
for herself and her son. And, after eating that last meal, she was prepared
to die.

But Elijah told her not to worry, that if she made a little cake for him,
she would also be able to feed herself and her son. In fact, he said, the
Lord God of Israel would provide meal and oil until the drought ended!

And she believed! She believed, did as Elijah said, and it all came true!

This is just amazing! This woman—without a provider, without food,
from a foreign territory, without hope—believed! She gave and was
provided for!

Oh, poof! That's just fantasy, make-believe, one of those miracle
stories you can't take literally! But why is that particular fantasy in the
Bible again and again? She gave and was provided for!

And, you know, *we've* had it happen to us—little miracles of *amazing* power. Yes, look again at what is fundamentally happening in the Gospel passage. Jesus shifted attention from planning and calculating our lives to surrendering them on faith. He was freeing us from appropriateness to willingness to free us from the letter of the law for the point of it all.

Yes, the message of the gospel is not condemnation but invitation. Invitation to the fullness and happiness of meaningful relationship and purpose. If Christ wanted to judge and guilt trip, why would he invite suffering on himself? What is the model he provided? Not one of judgment, but one of sacrifice.

You know, really, I think we're very much like the widow in the Mark passage: insecure, searching, vulnerable, down to our last two coins of faith. Even when we seem to have it made or others think we have it all together.

That was the position Ignatius found himself in as he faced heroic martyrdom in the first century after Christ's death. Ignatius seemed to have had it made. He was bishop of the church in Antioch, condemned to death for his work and beliefs by the Roman authorities. And, as he passed through other towns in Asia Minor on his way to Rome, members of the local churches would praise him and adulate him for courage in his impending martyrdom. But Ignatius was worried. *Worried* that— despite having it made, despite being able to meet his death in a respectable style—he would not die as a disciple.

"I do not think of myself entitled," he wrote to the church in Tralles, "condemned as I am, to command you like an Apostle. Now I must more than ever be afraid and not pay attention to those who flatter me. For those who talk to me scourge me. I am glad to suffer, but I do not know whether I am worthy."

That's where we often find ourselves, isn't it? Deep inside we are struggling, searching, vulnerable. We are not sure that, with *all* our efforts, we really have been able to make sense of the world and get the most out of life. We are like widows.

Ignatius sensed the reversal of the gospel message. He wrote ahead to the Roman church, "The ends of the earth and the kingdoms of this world will do me no good. It is better for me to die in Jesus Christ than to be king of the ends of the earth. . . . I am in search of Him who died for us. I want Him who rose for our sake. Childbirth is upon me. Excuse me, brethren. Do not hinder my coming to life."

That's the issue in our Scripture lesson today: coming to life. It is an invitation to let ourselves go of our own solutions and neat little plans for the alleged good life, and thus to be empty for the marvelous work of the Spirit.

The issue before us is not even being poor. You know, we can make a virtue of being poor and still miss the invitation. In fact, not only can we idealize poverty, blessed with the proper text, but also we can overlook the fact that persons in poverty also suffer from bitterness, resentment, and idolatry of the gods of materialism and self-importance.

No, the good news is an invitation to a kind of childbirth.

The widow at the treasury is the biblical image of emptiness before God. Because to be empty is to have capacity—capacity to be filled. Having been rid of everything, having stood empty and widow-like before God, one is able to receive everything—meaning and joy and unparalleled freedom—as a gift! Such a person is rich *because* she has just placed her last coin in the tray.

Now, that's a tough order to fill alone! Possible, but tough! But we have each other. That's what the church is about: to struggle together, to gain solace, and to celebrate the many gifts of caring and reaching out that we *do* accomplish in this world. The church is a place where we *can* confess together our shortcomings and needs without getting jumped on or embarrassed; a place where we *can* experience the incredible exhilaration of that amazing Spirit moving through our lives.

John Henry Jowett tells about an epitaph to a very dedicated, untiring, special person which he spotted in a graveyard outside a small village. It read: "She Hath Done What She Couldn't."

That's what happened to the widow of Zarephath when she was touched by the witness of Elijah: She Hath Done What She Couldn't.

That's what happened to the widow at the treasury who gave her last money: She Hath Done What She Couldn't.

That was what happens to the community in Christ's church when it is kissed by the breath of God: She Hath Done What She Couldn't.

This is the good news of Christ who has suffered and died just like we do. "There are angels in those lives, and I can set them free!"

> *Be* thou my vision, O Lord of my heart
> Naught be *all* else to me, save that *thou* art
> Thou my *best* thought, by day or by night
> Waking or sleeping, thy presence my light.

Appendix 6:
Examples of Written Styles of Preaching by Students at Allen Temple Baptist Church

Terminal Indifference
Paul Q. Rigmaiden

Prayer: O Lord, may this sermon be acceptable to you. Amen.
Scripture: Revelation 3:14-22.

As a result of regional stability brought to Asia Minor by the Roman Empire, Laodicea was a wealthy commercial city. It was refounded in 250 BC by Antiochus II and named after his wife, Laodice.

Laodicea was renowned for three things: it was a center for banking and high finance; it was so rich that, after an earthquake in AD 61, it rebuilt itself without outside help. The people of Laodicea took great pride in their material wealth; but we all know that money can't buy love, life, nor a spot in heaven. Laodicea was know for its textile industry, mainly for its black, glossy wool. Laodicean clothes represented the height of luxury in those days; but we all know that, no matter how many clothes we have, we can't hide ourselves nor our lives from the ever-seeing eye of God. Finally, Laodicea was a center for medical research and physical healing. It was highly regarded for *kollurion,* an effective salve for eye problems. But, of course, we all know that all the medical experts in the world cannot create life as God did in the beginning; nor can they give life to the dead. Yes, Laodicea was a wealthy, successful place; but its people were apparently so vain and proud of themselves that they felt they didn't need God.

But, for all its paved streets, gilded chariots (Cadillacs, Mercedes, El Dorados, and Sevilles), designer togas, money, and medicine, the church in Laodicea, like its water supply that came from distant hot springs, was lukewarm, indifferent to the message of Christ Jesus.

Yes, the city was rich and its people were proud, smug, and satisfied with their accomplishments in the material world. So much so that the

Christian church established there by the apostle Paul had become ambivalent, lackadaisical, uninspired, and halfhearted when it came to the message of Christ Jesus. They were, like many of us, too busy to be worried with Jesus; too busy to recognize that it was by God's loving grace that they were alive and had the things they had; too busy to recognize or remember that the hand which herded the stars into energy-filled galaxies sent someone to earth one day as Jesus Christ, Son of the Living God, so that we sin-encrusted humans could be saved from certain destruction (John 3:16).

Laodicea, the lukewarm church, the indifferent church, the only church in the Revelation that Jesus, in his amen form, his Holy Spirit form, said nothing good about! He said that because of their indifference they were like vomit, to be spat out of the mouth, useless to Jesus. How many times have we said to ourselves: "Man, I got it made! Got me a nice house, a nice car, nice clothes, a nice job, and ooo-weee!" Everything in our lives can cause us to be seen as spiritual vacuum-heads, naked, blind, and distasteful to God. Yes, we spend so much of our time keeping up with the "latest" or pursuing sensual pleasures that we forget about or try to ignore the real needs of our families, communities, and the rest of the world. Jesus doesn't want us if we aren't on fire for him, if we aren't committed to him. There's an old song called "All or Nothing at All." Well, that's the way it is with Jesus. He wants us—all of us—for our own good.

The blood of the Laodiceans had very strong properties, very strong genes: just think—there might be one sitting next to you right now or, even worse, there might be one sitting the same spot you're sitting in. When we say, "Who needs church?" or "Who needs religion or God or Jesus Christ? I have everything I need, and I got it all by myself!" we're suffering from the kind of selfishness that causes us to pretend God doesn't exist. We ignore the nudgings in our hearts and minds when we're in a particular situation and simply do what we *feel* like doing, right or wrong, fair or unjust. We often hurt our relationship with God because we spend so much time adding up the things we've done rather than counting our blessings and thanking God for them. And, yes, we frequently get so involved with rules, regulations, and other artifical procedures and processes that we forget about God and his Son, Jesus. "I ain't got the time! I ain't interested! I'm too busy counting the money from the offering to hear the sermon!" or, "The constitution says we're supposed to do things this way, Pastor!" or, "Pastor, your faith is nice, but we can't afford this right now!" Yes, the defiantly indifferent ones say these kinds of things. They place conditions on their relationship to God. Yes, when we come to church in this indifferent way, this uncommitted way, the sermons, songs, and Scriptures simply pass through our heads because we're too busy worrying about whether we should wear the blue suit or the brown suit tomorrow; or, if we'll be able to use those backstage passes at the next rock concert; or, if we should wear a monkey suit to the costume party; or, we think: "Hey! Who is that man (woman) over there? He (she) is so fine! What is your name, Honey?" And, even worse, we sit in the services wishing for the sermon to end because we just "don't care about none of this mess!"

Jesus tells us that, as a remedy for our indifference, we should turn to God (through him!) so we that will become spiritually rich, pure, and able to more easily see and do the truth.

Jesus loves us. And that means that, even if we're punished or even if our guilt allows us to suffer for our aloofness or our indifference toward him, he continues to love us!

Yes, Jesus stands at the door of our personalities. He's patiently waiting for us to let him into our lives, our hearts. He's knocking, waiting for commitment; waiting for the green light; waiting for us.

Yes, he rewards us, too, because he said—(Rev. 3:21, KJV, should be read or recited at this point.)

Conclusion/Exhortation

Because Jesus wants us, not in name only, Jesus calls us:

To work for him!
To minister to the sick and incarcerated!
To fight injustice!
To work for a world order based on love!
To lay our burdens at his feet!
To believe in him!
To trust in him!
To spread love wherever we may go!

Let him in! He's calling, knocking, waiting, and loving!!

(At this stage of the sermon, additional comments, exhortation, words of comfort and encouragement would be added to the message by the workings of the Holy Spirit.)

What's Your Story?
(Jer. 28:1-17)
Jini Robinson

Questions: What informs you? What reason lies behind your actions? What's your story? What do you believe? Hananiah and Jeremiah were both prophets in Jerusalem. They both foresaw the captivity of Jerusalem by the Babylonian king Nebuchadnezzer, which occurred in 587 BC. They both spoke of a yoke, that frame that was placed over oxen and other beasts of burden to enable them to pull the plow. Yokes were also put on human beings as they were taken into slavery; and the yoke was a symbol of captivity and exile. Hananiah broke the wooden yoke-bars that the prophet Jeremiah wore, declaring, "Thus says the Lord of hosts, the God of Israel: I have broken the yoke of the king of Babylon. Within two years [the captivity and exile will be ended]" (Jer. 28:2-3, RSV).

"[Not so]," says Jeremiah. And, replacing the wooden yoke with an unbreakable iron yoke, he declared, "Thus says the Lord, You have broken wooden bars, but I will make in their place bars of iron" (v. 13, RSV).

The Babylonian captivity would last seventy years, not two. Jeremiah 29 records Jeremiah's advice to the people to marry in Babylon, build houses, and plant gardens, to even seek the welfare of the city because the generation that was taken captive would never return to Jerusalem.

What was happening? Two prophets said, "Thus saith the Lord," then proceeded to tell different stories. Jeremiah said that Hananiah lied; and, indeed, the seventy-year captivity proves that he did. But why? Was it a deliberate lie?

Probably not. You see, there were some contrasts between Jeremiah and Hananiah. They hung their hats on different beliefs about life. Hananiah represented a group of Temple prophets who were informed by what we will call nationalism, or the David-Zion story.

The story line for nationalists was told in this way: God has promised to uphold his city, Jerusalem, and his chosen people. David's kingdom would never cease and his people would be preserved forever. It was a familiar story. Had not Habakkuk said, "The Lord is in his holy temple" (2:20). How could the enemy destroy the place where the Lord dwelt? Had not the prophet Nahum told Judah, "Keep your feasts . . . fulfill your vows, for never again shall the wicked come against you" (2:15, RSV) Zephaniah had boldly declared, "Do not fear, O Zion; let not your hands grow weak. The Lord, your God, is in your midst, a warrior who gives victory" (3:16-17, RSV).

What's your story, Hananiah? Well, he answers from history with a shallow understanding of God's plan. He expected God to have an earthly messiah, not unlike King David. He didn't know that our God could use captivity to preserve his people; for when we are in trouble, we draw closer to God. He didn't understand that God works in mysterious ways his mighty wonders to perform.

You see, there was another story, and it was the story that Jeremiah believed. W. Lee Humphreys in his book *Crisis and Story* calls this other story the Moses-Sinai story. It had to do with the covenant relationship, the love relationship between God and his people and their love relationship between one another. It was the story that the eighth-century prophet, Amos, believed when he recalled how God had brought his people up out of Egypt. Therefore, they were not to cheat one another, or rip each other off; but, instead, "Let justice roll down like waters, and righteousness like an ever-flowing stream" (Amos 5:24, RSV). Jeremiah's story was like Hosea's, who said, "When Israel was a child, I loved him" (11:1, RSV). Jeremiah's story was like David's, who wrote, "[Not temples, not cities, not fortresses or sacrifices and burnt offerings]," Oh, no, these are not what the Lord requires, but "a broken and a contrite heart" (Ps. 51:17).

Well, nobody liked Jeremiah's story. The prophets of nationalism were more popular. Even Jeremiah despised the telling of the captivity and long Exile. But he had no choice. He had to tell the story, for he said: "The word of the Lord has become for me a reproach and derision all day long. If I say 'I will not mention him, or speak any more in his name", . . . a burning fire shut up in my bones, and I am weary with holding it in" (20:9, RSV).

Yes, Exile would once again bring the people of God back to him from their straying ways. They would know, like their forefathers, how it would feel to come out of the wilderness, leaning on the Lord. They would be able to sing a new song that, if it had not been for the Lord on our side, where would we be?

Well, what's your story—yours and mine? It's Black History Month. How are we coming along as a people? You see, we have to be very careful because it's easy to become like Hananiah. In effect, he based his prophecy on the wrong point of view about God. Sometimes I wonder if we don't have the wrong point of view about life. They tell me that if Black America were to be counted as a separate nation, we'd be one of the wealthiest nations in the world, with respect to our cumulative annual earnings. I don't want to be too hard on us, but I can't help but wonder what story, what underlying presupposition, if you will, informs those Koreans, those Southeast Asians who have been here less than a generation, yet are buying up all of the businesses in our neighborhoods.

Well, it must be a family story. From what I can see, everybody in the family goes to work—they help each other. Even young people are brought up to be responsible. They seem to understand that there is a time for everything, and so they get their lessons and come home and work in the business. You can see them at Merritt College, eating rice out of a bowl. Black youngsters are often laughing at them. "Why don't they buy hamburgers and French fries like everyone else?" But next year, the Asian will have the last laugh, as we go to their stores to buy our hamburger meat and potatoes. It seems that theirs is a story of frugality, mutual sacrifice, and delayed gratification.

What's your story, Black America? It used to resemble the togetherness of these new immigrants. We could do it again. God help us to slay jealousy, mistrust, and, above all, adult irresponsibility in the rearing of our children. We have to teach good values to our children. And we have to teach by example as well as by precept.

I pray that God will help us to realize the importance of strong family units. We've been having too many stories that read like *Peyton Place* and *All My Children*. Christians! Christians! I make an appeal to you, in the name of Jesus, to be forceful about these values that we hold dear. Fight for the survival of your family! It's worth it! If you need counseling, get counseling. Don't be too proud. If you need the fellowship of other Christian families, make yourself available for that fellowship. Fight for your family! Don't let these bad winds blow you over! Let's have a story of togetherness, trust, love, and mutual prosperity.

Now I'd like to say a word about the church, as I prepare to close. I'm not talking about the church universal or the local church but about you and me, the individuals who make up the collective body of Christ. You see, it starts with you. It starts with me. We can't have a strong family without strong individuals who are strong in the Lord! We can't have a strong people, loving, trusting, and working with each other unless we're strong in the Lord. It starts with the redeemed soul. O yes, it does! It continues as babes in Christ mature in the knowledge and wisdom of holiness. And, you know, I've discovered in my own Christian journey—I won't talk about anyone else's—that it is easy to become like Hananiah. Yes, Hananiah had the wrong point of view about God. And so do we. So often we think that God is a spiritualized Dr. Feelgood. O yes, we do. We believe when we can feel his presence; then, in between feelings, we wander in deserts of doubt and faithlessness. We're so big on feelings that we mistake them for fact. Oh, what a clever deception of Satan's, for who would deny the validity of his feelings. But I came to tell you a story this evening. And it's all about that which is real beyond the evidence of our feelings. You see:

> Three men were walking on a wall,
> Feeling, Faith and Fact,
> When Feeling got an awful fall,
> And Faith was taken back.

> So close was Faith to Feeling
> He stumbled and fell, too
> But Fact remained
> And pulled Faith back
> And Faith brought Feeling, too.

You need some facts in your life to help you discern the deceptions of feeling, to help you get the story right. Fact is that "God so loved the world, that he gave his only begotten Son, that whosoever believeth in him should not perish, but have everlasting life" (John 3:16). The fact is that the overwhelming love of God causes us to love ourselves and our neighbors as ourselves. The fact is that love brings togetherness. The fact is that Jesus saves, strengthens, and preserves. He lifts up the broken-hearted; he restores the lost. Jesus befriends the lonely. He comforts the despairing. The fact is that I wouldn't want to live without Jesus. I don't know how I could make it from day to day without him. I believe my story would have had a tragic ending without the love of the Savior. The fact is that Jesus is all the world to me, my life, my joy, my all. No feeling can overcome the fact of Jesus' presence. This is my story! Church, is this your story? Jesus is my reality! He is my strength from day to day. He is the fact, hallelujah! Praise the Lord!

Amen!

To the Church at Smyrna: "Hold On!"
(Revelation 2:8-11)
Eugene Williams

Jesus' message to the church of Smyrna, by way of the apostle John, was one of acknowledgment, compliment and support, warning, encouragement, and promise.

He acknowledged that they were workers dealing in tribulation and experiencing earthly poverty. He complimented and supported them by telling them that they were rich spiritually. That was what counted. *Spiritually rich* tells me that the church at Smyrna had some strong prayer warriors. *Spiritually rich* tells me that somebody there knew what it meant to love the Lord God with all their heart, all their soul, and with all their strength, and "lean not unto thine own understanding" (Prov. 3:5). The church at Smyrna was a working church. It was involved in community affairs, and its leaders were active in commercial trade for goods and services for its members and its community; for the city of Smyrna was, in biblical times, one of the largest and busiest commercial centers of the entire region of Asia Minor and the Aegean Sea. It was an active church, an involved church, a church aware that faith without works is dead, a church aware of what Jesus meant when he said, "But he that is greatest among you shall be your servant" (Matt. 23:11). John's message of support and compliment also brought with it a warning, for God is always conscious of obstacles in our way. If we are tuned in and have slowed down or speeded up enough to hear, he will warn us of our opposition. The church at Smyrna had two main oppositions: one was cults and various mystical black magic groups which were extremely hostile to the church; and slander and more hostility came to the church by a group of Jews whom Jesus said were hypocrites, phonies, and not to be feared. Through all of this and the intense persecution that was to come upon the church at Smyrna, Jesus' message to Smyrna was: be faithful, Smyrna, even until death; for I, Jesus said, "will give thee a crown of life" (v. 10).

This message was strength to the church at Smyrna, and it revitalized and recharged their faith. They knew God was with them through the rough, tough days ahead. It's a good, comforting feeling to know that

God is with you, with us, through difficult times. And a word from the Lord by way of a friend, a Christian brother or sister, a smile, a hug, and a kiss can help us make it through the day.

Well, brothers and sisters, on this glorious historical occasion, what can this message to the church at Smyrna tell us? Well, God's presence has truly been with the Allen Temple Family through sixty-four years in Oakland—from a storefront with twenty borrowed chairs to a glorious temple of worship, to a membership of nearly three thousand, with a nationally known Christian giant as a leader. This is truly God's acknowledgment, compliment, and support for the Allen Temple ministry in Oakland, in this state, and throughout this nation. Now, the warning is that Satan is angry; and his spirits consider it a privilege to shoot at you, hassle you, and throw you off course. But, remember Jesus' message to the church at Smyrna: Hold On! Hold on because, in times like these, this world needs a Savior and a Lord, and God's work is carried out and manifested through the church whose Rock, Founder, Doctor, and Lawyer is Jesus Christ. Hold on because, with family breakups at an all-time high, with teenage problems of drug abuse, crime, teenage pregnancies and VD running rampant in all kinds of forms, God's church is so needed to heal sin-sick souls; straighten out confused minds; turn cold, unforgiving hearts to loving hearts; to bring down puffed up, sophisticated, snobbish egos and personalities; and to teach and train men to be men and women to be women. As John delivered the message to the church at Smyrna, Jesus is saying today: Hold on to God's unchanging hand! Keep the faith! Don't become sidetracked by cults and groups appealing to your emotions and impulses, bringing instant answers, instant satisfaction, and instant success. Take that steady, close, sure, and prayerful closer walk with God. The church at Smyrna had what is considered the third recorded martyr after that of Stephen recorded in Acts 6. Their leader, Bishop Polycarp, near the age of eighty-six, was burned alive after the city's council ordered him to denounce his faith and belief in Christ Jesus or be killed. But Bishop Polycarp, as well as James, Peter, and Paul, did not renounce his faith and belief in Christ and took his conviction that we are not ashamed of the gospel of Jesus Christ. For it's the power unto salvation to everyone that believes it.

Brothers and sisters, hold on! God will see you through! God has not built you up just to let you down! God has not directed national attention to the Allen Temple urban ministry and brought together this warm, positive body of believers in a cold, negative non-believing world for nothing.

God has not brought us across the Atlantic through many dangers, toils, and snares to have us give up, shut up, freak out, and burn out! Hold on! For we have "come this far by faith, leaning on the Lord, trusting in his holy Word" through slavery; trusting in his holy Word through the Civil War, World War I, through World War II, through "Jim Crow" laws, through the Korean War, Vietnam, the Civil Rights Era of the late fifties and sixties, through the relaxed late sixties and early seventies, and through the shocking late seventies to the present. You can't turn around; I can't turn around; we can't turn around because we've come this far by faith, leaning on the Lord!

Hold on, church, hold on! God will see you through!

Persistence Rewarded
(Luke 18:1-8)
Haywood Harvey

Introduction

Those who stubbornly and constantly continue along their course in the face of opposing odds and objections are defined as being persistent purveyors. William W. McDermet, III, detailed the following illustration in *The Upper Room:*

> Suppose you need to cut down a tree in your back yard—it need not be a tree, nor does it have to be in your back yard. In order to proceed, you count the number of blows it will take for the tree to fall victim to the relentless will of the chopper's resolve. . . . let's say 136 well-directed strikes. And if you were to ask a toddler which of the blows caused the tree to topple, he would insist that the credit be given to the last chop. However, the tree would still be just as majestically standing if it had not been for the first blow, the second blow and the subsequent interim blows, strikes and chops.

A parable is a simple story told to illustrate or teach a moral truth. The above parable provides proof and insight about how we are to pray and how to interpret the many ways in which the Lord answers. Positive persistence is ever effective in everyday human interactions and relationships. God's ubiquitous nature pervades these human encounters enough that we sense his deeds and influences. To Jesus, prayer was the simple and plaintive outpouring of human need. Jesus—and Jesus knows—that prayer is oftentimes a tireless supplication.

When we persist in prayer, our patience is perfected, our humiliation is made more humble, and our many and myriad purposes are elucidated and clarified. Prayer must be free of all affectations, such as insincerity, selfishness, and vanity. The knock at times must be relentless, resounding, and resolute before the door swings open in acquiescence.

The point of the parable is that God truly wants to grant and give note to our requests. Pleading is unnecessary when we go to the Lord in honest and earnest efforts to obtain bread, jobs, justice, quiet jubilation, and human rights. According to Luke, Jesus' statement that all prayer will be answered was absolute. Jesus encouraged prayer. When prayer is desperate struggle, the ultimate struggle and battles are with ourselves.

Which blow felled the tree? The last one, without a doubt. But was the first one necessary? Blow for blow and chop for chop were necessary. Prayer will be as it is with the trees that need to come down—a consistent chopping away. Our prayers ascend and mingle with those of the multitudes of other praying humanity.

E. M. Bounds in his book, *Purpose in Prayer,* avers that

> the more praying there is in the world, the better the world will be, the mightier the forces against evil everywhere. Prayers outlive an age; they outlive a world. A man can pray better because of the prayers of the past. The secret of success in Christ's Kingdom is the ability to pray. The most important lesson we can learn is how to pray.

Therefore, we should pray with unwavering, unfaltering persistence.

What Is Prayer?

Prayer is as old as humanity, as universal as religion, and as instinctive as breathing. Praying is asking and receiving. It is a soliloquy directed to God. It is making one's needs known to God in overt and covert actions of faith. In Matthew 7:7, the Lord instructed the true believer to *ask, seek,* and *knock.* These three words cover the whole spectrum of prayer.

Prayer Is Seeking and Finding

When I am in doubt about the will of God with regard to a need, whether it be material or spiritual, then I am to persist in solemn and sincere supplication until my doubts have been resolved. This is the prayer of knowledge of the unrevealed will of God in a specific need (Col. 3:1; Jer. 29:12-13).

Prayer Is Asking and Receiving

When I know the will of God regarding a need, whether it is spiritual or material, I can ask and receive. This is prayer according to the *revealed* will of God (1 John 5:14-15).

Prayer Is Knocking and Opening

When we know the will of the Lord and yet we find the door does not give to our incessant calling, we are to knock and know that our knocking will cause the door to fall ajar, and then crack, and then give way to full opening of God's mysterious mercies. This is powerful, potent prayer—prayer for mountain-moving faith. Knocking prayer perseveres until the impossible becomes possible. This is miracle-working prayer (Matt. 17:14-21).

What This Parable Teaches

This Parable Does Not Teach Us to Pray

There is no need that it do so. As breathing and eating are instinctive actions of the body, prayer is instinctive action of the soul. We should not need to be told to pray. Prayer should be a natural reaction to glorious and glittering sunrises and sunsets. Thanks should be given for the old car that has taken you over many roads. Prayers are given for the courage you had when you did not lose heart; when you did not cave in to doubts, suspicions, fears, and follies. Don't use unanswered prayers as a reason to discontinue your monologues—for selfish, self-serving prayer is a monologue, not a dialogue with God. Rebuke and resist all opposition to answers that might suggest failure. Divine blood has bargained for us the right to receive answers. Faithless hearts and souls are useless to the Lord.

This Parable Teaches Us How to Pray

The point here is that earnestness and frequency, along with constancy and perseverance, enhance and embellish the importunity of prayer. This simply means that we should praise God daily. To omit daily prayer is like marching into raging battle leaving weapons and arms securely locked in the arsenal. It is like embarking on an endeavor without the essentials for finishing. It is a brakeless car . . . nails without a hammering tool. Succinctly put, there is little you can do without the proper fuel: prayer.

This Parable Teaches Persevering Prayer

Praying is trying travail. It is said that it is harder to pray than it is to minister the word of the Lord. Why is this so?

Somehow, we do not believe what we profess, nor do we feel what we say we feel. Sometimes we do not want what we wish or we use unsavory means to obtain that which we really don't need. In these human weaknesses lie the reasons for so many unanswered prayers. God can see through our vanities and vulgarities. Do we pray as we continue through the day, the week, the month, the year, the life? Do we offer silent prayers for our many blessings in our homes, while we are jogging or exercising, or coming and going from our places of employment? If we would pray until it resounded, as does the mighty rolling stream, change would come. The constant dripping of water will wear a hole in a rock. Only in perseverance in prayer can it bring its blessings down to us on this island Earth.

The Parable of the Persistent Widow

This widow seems to have been everywhere and was determined to get justice rendered unto her by the judge. The lady in question was without financial means, community influence. Simply put, the widow had no power. All women, much less our widow, have had few rights. However, this widow was persistent and believed that she would get the justice which she deserved. She followed the judge everywhere he went. She found him on the golf course, in his chambers, and in his court. She interrupted his chatter with colleagues, as well as his legal arguments, to obtain her justice. The cry was always the same as she waited at his door, at his car, at his church: "Give me legal protection from my opponent!" His friends begin to tease and ape him. They said among themselves and to him (there are those who merely think and offer no opinion): "You are so tough, hard, and adamant, yet you cannot free yourself from this haunting little old lady." This judge had a reputation of not fearing God or holding respect for any man. However, he met his match in the widow! So the judge said, "I'll give this widow her legal protection because her constant coming just wears me out."

We may expect persistence in prayer to succeed better with God than with people not because the means used are stronger in one case but because it has no adversity to overcome.

God is our Father and the forgiving Judge of our deeds and actions. He needs to be told of our needs only once. Repeated prayer is not intended to remind but to thank him. Tell God once and give thanks a million times. He will answer our requests in a way that will bring ultimate good and creative growth in our lives.

When we are besieged by problems and preoccupations, we must look at them from a positive perspective. For, out of tribulation, comes perseverance; from perseverance comes proven character; from proven character comes hope. Hope does not disappoint because the love of God has been passed out within the hearts through the Holy Spirit. My hope is in God, not in a solution to a problem.

Conclusion

Jesus knew that prayer is oftentimes a tireless supplication. He knew that the knock at times would seem to be relentless, resounding, and resolute. In this panoramic view of things aforementioned, Jesus encouraged prayer. And, again: which blow toppled the tree?

Our prayers have ascended and mingled with those of the multitudes of other praying masses of humanity. Therefore, we should pray with unfaltering persistence. God will answer our persistent knocking and continual asking in ways that we cannot envision. Persistence in prayer without the accompanying weaknesses of human frailties will cause doors to open and all prayers to be answered. We, as humans, do not and cannot understand the workings of our Lord. The doors will open when the knock and divine timing both are right—not before. Persistence assures and ensures that the doors will ultimately open.

The Most Dangerous People in the Church
(Matt. 13:24-30; 36-42)
Robert K. Gordon

Introduction

In spite of the presence of God, in spite of the activities of the saints, in spite of the struggles of the missionaries, in spite of the death of martyrs, in spite of all the heroisms of all the centuries, in spite of the causes of righteousness, *SIN* has not yet been driven out of one single nation, city, or community. It has not even been completely and perfectly exterminated in one single church in all the world. Go anywhere and you will find sin present.

"Show me a perfect church," one member says to another, "and I will join it."

The second member counters, "You will do nothing of the kind. What would you and I do in a perfect church? In the first place, such a church would not admit us. In the second place, such a church would be a tremendous embarrassment to us. And, in the third place, such a church would cease at once to be perfect, as soon as we joined it."

Despite sin, however, I believe that the church is the hope of the world; but, even in the church, there are tares growing among the wheat.

In this particular parable, Jesus was addressing what had been for centuries a perplexing problem. Three points are illustrated in this parable:

1. The coexistence of good and evil, the bewildering mixture of real and counterfeit wheat; the uncommitted rubbing elbows with the committed.
2. The problem for us of recognizing the good and the bad in the church.
3. The providence of God's method in managing the affairs of his church.

At one time in Jesus' ministry, the parables were his only method of speaking to the masses. As his enemies sought opportunities to accuse him, he resorted to these hard-to-understand illustrations. As one preacher has said, "Jesus' parables were 'spiritual baby talk.' "

A parable is a form of speaking that compares two objects for the purpose of teaching. In a parable, two truths are placed side-by-side. To some who hear, the truth will be hidden; but to others it, will be clear. The parables were an effective, figurative method of revealing truth to the spiritual and ready mind and, at the same time, of concealing its meaning from the spiritually blind and deaf (Matt. 13:11).

Christ came as Israel's King, and only after the Jews had rejected him did he change to the parable form of imparting spiritual truth. Those who rejected him were not to know the "mysteries of the kingdom of heaven."

Three Gospel writers record about thirty-one of Jesus' parables, and only a few of that number were explained or interpreted by him. The story of the wheat and the tares is one of the parables that Jesus expounded to his disciples.

Interpretation of the Wheat and the Tares

"Then Jesus sent the multitude away" (v. 36). After hearing the Master's sayings, many in the crowd went away no wiser than they came. It is said: think how many people go away from hearing a sermon with the *WORD* of grace in their ears, but not the *WORK* of grace in their hearts.

He that Sows the Good Seed Is Jesus

Whatever good seed there is in the world, it all comes from the hands of Christ and is of his sowing. Truths preached, graces planted, souls sanctified are good seed and all owing to Christ.

The Field Is the World of Humanity

Jesus came to save humanity, "For God so loved the world, that he gave his only begotten Son" (John 3:16). "The earth is the Lord's, and the fulness thereof" (Ps. 24:1).

The Good Seed Are the Children of God's Kingdom

The true saints—not in the profession only, as were the Jews, but in sincerity of heart—are the good seed. It is not enough to merely profess Christ, but you must possess him.

The Tares Are the Children of Satan

They are up to no good; they only destroy. They are the weeds and thistles in the garden, having the same rain, the same sunshine, and the same soil with the good plants but are good for nothing.

In the church, the tares represent the most dangerous people. It is not the unconfessed sinner outside the church who poses the greatest threat; it is the hypocrite within.

The Enemy Who Sowed the Tares Is the Devil

Satan is endeavoring to make the world his own by sowing his tares in it. The tares are planted while people are sleeping. Satan watches for all opportunities to sift and devour the good. The Christians, therefore, need to be sober and watchful at all times.

The Harvest Is the End of the World

At harvesttime, the Great Judgment Day, everybody reaps as he or she has sowed; every person's ground, seed, skill, and industry will be manifested. What's done in the dark will come to the light at the Judgment Day, if tares are not led before that time to repentance.

The Reapers Are the Heavenly Angels

The angels, dispatched by God at the great Judgment Day, will have the specific task of gathering the weeds (tares) and bundling them together. The angels will be given the wisdom and the insight to distinguish the tares from the wheat. We, as moral beings, do not possess enough wisdom and insight to determine who are the dangerous people in the local church. People look on the outward appearance, but God judges the heart of persons.

The Parable and the Church

Some people have the meaning of the church confused. The church is not a dormitory for sleepers; it is an institution for workers. It is not a rest camp; it is a front-line trench to fight the battle with the Lord's help against Satan. When speaking of the church, I am not referring to the four walls of a building, but, rather, about the company or assembly of baptized believers in Christ Jesus.

In every church we have basically two kinds of people. It makes all the difference for now and eternity which group you are in. The purpose and challenge of this message are to liberate people from the "tares" category to the "wheat" category.

The "wheat" in the church I am calling the "Insiders." The "tares" in the church I am calling the "Outsiders." The Outsiders (tares), represent the most dangerous people in the church. Only two people have the prerogative of determining which group you are identified with—Jesus Christ and you.

The Insiders and the Outsiders may often look alike, sing alike, pray a prayer alike, and both believe in Jesus Christ. The Outsiders look and act much like the Insiders. Since both look so much alike, you may ask, What are the differences?

The Outsiders are within the church but are outside a deep personal relationship with Christ as Lord of their lives. The Outsiders believe that Jesus is the Savior of the world but have never come to know him as the Lord of their lives. They have never made a complete commitment of all they have. The Outsiders have not had an intimate, impelling, and indwelling experience of Christ as Lord.

The Outsiders are "some-timey" Christians who delight only in a few minutes thrills with God on Sunday mornings, while for the remainder of the day and the rest of the week they do not become involved in an outreach ministry. Some Outsiders are only interested in a "spiritual intercourse" with the Creator on a Sunday morning for they don't have time for him the rest of the week.

An Outsider says, "I run my own life! I do my own thing whenever I please! I control my destiny! I am capable of making my own decisions!" He or she says, "I did it my way!" instead of saying, "I did it God's way!"

The Outsiders are reluctant to make any commitment because they are afraid that they will be unable to keep it. They are *not* leaning and depending on the Lord. The tares have not learned to lay their all on the altar of sacrifice. Their hearts the Spirit does not control. They have not discovered for themselves that, "You can only be blest and have peace and sweet rest as you yield to God your body and soul."

The Outsiders may be working anywhere in the church: in the choirs, in the board of Christian education, in the church Sunday School, on the deacon or deaconness board, on the usher board—just anywhere.

They are dangerous people because they want to do God's work on their own strength and intellect.

As long as the Outsiders attempt to control their own lives, they will continue to have problems and to be problems. They do not allow the church to move beyond their limited experiences. The Outsiders are really the stumbling blocks to the progress of the church. They seldom pray, except in times of crisis. They are not interested in attending Bible classes to learn more about the Word of God. Most of all, the Outsiders fail to have that perfect love for others. They are just pretenders, sounding brass and tinkling cymbals.

The first group, the wheat, are called the Insiders. The Insiders realize the power of Christ in their lives. They trust him with their frustrations and fears. The Insiders have tried Jesus for peace, for answers to life's problems, and for direction. The Insiders have found out that he never fails.

The Insiders proclaim with conviction that:

> The Lord is my Shepherd,
> I have everything I need;
> not position, prestige nor
> power, but the Lord is
> my Shepherd. I'll trust Him
> for everything.

If the Master is truly in your hearts, you, the Insiders, can say with blessed assurance that Jesus is mine. He is my All and All!

I have heard many people sing a hymn from their lips; but I can feel the spirit and sincerity from the heart of the Insiders when such songs as:

> Guide me, O thou great Jehovah,
> Pilgrim through this barren land;
> I am weak, but thou art mighty,
> Hold me with thy pow'rful hand.

In this parable of describing the Insiders and the Outsiders, Jesus had wanted his disciples to ask: Am I the wheat or the weed in the church, in the field? Today, we must ask ourselves that same question and also ponder these questions:

> Am I a pillar or a sleeper? Am I a wing or a weight?
> Am I a promoter or a provoker? Am I a doer or a deadhead?
> Am I a supporter or a sponger? Am I a helper or a hinderer?
> Am I a spectator or a participator?
> Am I a campaigner or a camper?

Conclusion

This parable offers hope. If you want to change your status from a do-nothing follower to a dynamic follower of Christ, he says that there is still opportunity for you now before the angels come to bundle up the tares and cast them into the furnace of hell.

No other person on earth is qualified to judge and separate the wheat and tares. At the great Judgment Day, only Jesus and his angels will part the good seed from the spoiled ones.

There are four simple steps in changing over from a tare to a wheat grain. The first step is that you must *admit Christ.* Let the Lord into your heart by opening the door and receiving him into your life. Romans 10:9 shows you how: "If thou shalt confess with thy mouth the Lord Jesus, and shalt believe in thine heart that God hath raised him from the dead, thou shalt be saved."

The second step is to *commit* your life to him. Psalm 37:5 says, "Commit thy way unto the Lord; trust also in him, and he shall bring it to pass." A commitment involves a resolution to go all the way with Jesus. Not just on a Sunday morning, but every day staying in touch with the Savior of the world.

The third step is that you must *submit.* Surrender your will and desires to the Lord. James 4:7-8 says, "Submit yourselves therefore to God. Resist the devil, and he will flee from you. Draw near to God and he will draw near to you" (RSV).

There is a nonbiblical adage that goes: "If you make one step, God will make two." The problem with this approach is that too many people only make one step—and go no further. Living for God entails a continual daily walking with him in order to draw near.

The last step is that you must *transmit.* Too many Outsiders are trying to solve their own problems and have not discovered the Problem Solver. They need to do like countless thousands have done: "Take your burdens to the Lord and leave them there."

"O, what needless pain we bear; All because we do not carry Ev'rything to God in prayer!"

Appendix 7:
Examples of Oratory and Style in Modern Black Preachers

Songs of Hope from Dungeons of Despair
(Acts 16:25)
J. Alfred Smith, Jr.

(Delivered to the Music Conference of the American Baptist Churches of the West. First Baptist Church, Sacramento, California, January 28, 1983)

To experience music is to be captivated by one of the most beautiful phenomena in creation. Music travels gracefully through the air, moving from soul to soul, warming hearts and stimulating minds. Music expresses the subtleties of thought and feeling which words only cloud or corrupt.

Music has the unique ability to intertwine with the elements of nature, to harmonize with its environs, and to reflect and sometimes alter the background on which it is cast. No wonder Giuseppe Mazzini called music, "The harmonious voice of creation, an echo of the invisible world."

Music moves in, around, and through the very fabric of life. Lullabies bring smiles of peace to the faces of crying infants, while brassy fanfares raise crowds to cheer and shout in giant sports arenas. From ancient history until now, all people in all lands have enjoyed the blessing of music.

In ancient Greece, a writer did not lift a pen until consulting one of the nine muses. For the Papago Indians of America, music was the most precious of possessions. The Sufi mystics of the East used music to enter into spiritual states of ecstasy, and communities in Africa used drum music to communicate with one another long before Alexander Graham Bell invented the telephone. Yes, all people in all lands have become enamored with music. That is why Henry Wadsworth Longfellow could justly assert, "Music is the universal language of mankind.

However, it is with proud prejudice and unregrettable bias that I inform you that the greatest music of all is the music of the church! Yes, church music is special. It is not merely music for music's sake, nor has it the sole purpose of moving us to aesthetic appreciation. Rather, church music is awakened and animated by a divine touch which lifts the music and its partakers to higher ground.

I agree with the late African-American composer, Duke Ellington, who said:

> Sacred music in all of its forms offers a universal point of meeting. But what makes the music sacred is not a rigid category nor a fixed pattern of taste. The sole criterion is whether or not the hearts of the musicians and the listener are offered in response and devotion to God.

Therefore, it matters not whether we speak of the hymns of Ambrose or Isaac Watts, whether we look to the sacred oratorios of Bach or Handel, whether we relate to the gospels of Thomas Dorsey or the spirituals of the antebellum South, one truth holds universally: worship music is a sincere response of the heart to the glory and grace of God.

Because of its divine connection, it is essential that we view religious music from a posture of humility and reverence. We must always be aware that the fundamental goals of religious music are to worship God and to minister to God's people. These two goals reflect the very spirit of Jesus' two great Commandments to us, that (1) we should love God with all our heart, soul, and mind; and (2) we should love our neighbors as ourselves.

When we sing joyous praises to God, we are exemplifying our love to him. When we sing songs that provide comfort and hope to our listeners, we are demonstrating love to our neighbors. Love must be central to the ministry of music. Sometimes we become so wrapped up in the routine and mechanics of the music task that we lose sight of the fact that church music must be a channel for love. Unfortunately, some of Satan's choicest dens of dissension and division are in the choir lifts of our churches. The fiery flames of hell all but rise up on Sunday morning because choir members are feuding with one another, ministers are infuriated with directors, directors are upset with prima donna soloists, soloists are angry with musicians, and love is nowhere to be found.

I am reminded of a story told by Helen Salem Rizk about a New England church experiencing internal difficulties. To state it mildly, there was a difference of opinion within the congregation. An argument of an unspecified nature had grown to such an extent that the choir became rebellious. The pastor received word that the choir was going to express its displeasure by refusing to sing on the following Sunday. To avert the anticipated trouble, the pastor stood up in the pulpit on the next Sunday morning during worship service and announced the opening hymn as "We're Marching to Zion." After reading through the first verse, he turned to the choir and requested that they lead in the singing of the second verse which began: "Let those refuse to sing Who never knew our God." Needless to say, not a single soul refused to sing. Worship participants must always be ready to channel love. If we love the Lord, then we must "let our joys be known." If we love the Lord, then we must "Join in a song of sweet accord, And thus surround the throne." Anything that detracts worshipers from channeling love to God and to neighbors has no place in God's church. Whatever the detraction, it is too petty to be brought into the service of worship.

Church music must be viewed as a ministry of love. It is not separate from ministry, nor is it juxtaposed with ministry. Church music is a vital, organic form of ministry. This music rains down upon the parched souls of despair and raises seeds of hope for desolate souls.

This music, this wellspring of living water, revived Paul and Silas so that they could overcome a distressing condition. Paul and Silas were savagely beaten, locked in chains, and thrust into prison. But there, during the midnight hour, the darkest point in time, a time of hurt and sorrow, an hour of apparent frustration and travail, Paul and Silas sang praises unto God.

This story serves as an example to us that when we encounter the worst of experiences, when we feel physically debilitated, spiritually weakened, and emotionally depressed, and when the lighted forces of good appear to be snuffed out by the diabolical forces of evil, it is then that we should be able to celebrate most by singing praises to God.

Father Henry Nouwen explains why celebration should not just be confined to our good days. He says:

> Celebration is only possible through the deep realization that life and death are never found completely separate. Celebration can only really come about when fear and love joy and sorrow, tears and smiles can exist together. Celebration is the acceptance of life and a constantly increasing awareness of its preciousness.

We who are of the Afro-American Christian experience can identify with what this Dutch priest is saying. Reverend William McClain, a Black Methodist pastor, tells us: "The Black worship tradition . . . urges worshippers to turn themselves loose into the existential here and now where joy and travail mingle together as part of the reality of God's creation."

No wonder our slave forebears could sing the true but seemingly contradictory words, "Nobody knows the trouble I've seen, Glory Hallelujah." Despite pain and suffering, they praised the Lord. Despite heartache and heartbreak, poverty and oppression, they praised the Lord. Despite losses of freedom and family, identity and history, they praised the Lord.

They praised Him in the sanctuaries of their hearts.
They praised Him for His mighty Acts.
They praised Him according to His excellent greatness
And though they had their musical instruments
taken away, and were not permitted to dance His
praises, everyone who had breath praised The
Lord.

The great scholar, W. E. B. DuBois, explained how praise could come forth from songs of sorrow. He wrote: "Through all the sorrow of the sorrow songs, there breathes a hope, a faith in the ultimate justice of things."

This breath of hope which exists in the midst of sorrow is not limited to Black American Christians. This living hope-faith is shared by all who lay claim to that "Old rugged cross, the emblem of suffering and shame." For it was out of the context of suffering that some of the church's great music was written.

Hymn writer Martin Rinkart was surrounded by seventeenth-century war and pestilence, yet he celebrated by writing, "Hallelujah, Love, Thanks, and Praise." The great churchman Martin Luther, though persecuted, stood firmly and after reflecting on the Psalm 46 wrote "A Mighty Fortress Is Our God." Elizabeth Prentiss celebrated in her ill health by writing "More Love to Thee, O Christ," while Fannie Crosby, despite her blindness, wrote "Blessed Assurance, Jesus Is Mine."

One of the great musical stories of all time centers around an experience of Mrs. C. D. Martin who, with her husband, was visiting Mr. and Mrs. Doolittle of Elmira, New York. The Doolittles were both incurably crippled but were of good cheer. This astonished the Martins who inquired as to how they could have such joy. Mrs. Doolittle responded with pride, "His eye is on the sparrow, and I know He watches me!" Mrs.

Martin was so taken by the response that she went home and that same day arranged those touching words into one of the great hymns of all time.

All through church history, God's people have looked beyond the dark clouds of suffering to the bright skies of hope, as they sang praises to God. That is why Afro-American churchmen feel special kinship with those European and Anglo-American hymn writers who have known similar trials and tribulations. Thus, the English writer, Isaac Watts, is fondly referred to as Dr. Watts, for his hymns carry the telltale signs of someone who has emerged from the dark, dusky dungeons of despair to hold up the name of Jesus. You see, Dr. Watts was stricken by a fever that left him an invalid until his death, still he wrote "Joy to the World! The Lord Is Come" and hundreds of other hymns.

Contemporary Christians must continue, in the tradition of Paul and Silas, to sing processionals of praises to God, even in the bleakest hours. As we worship in our churches, we must remember to give our all. No matter how difficult times may become, we must be ready with a song. We cannot base our commitment on the amount of popular support we gain; but, rather, we must be prepared to sing God's wonderful praises instantly, in season and out of season. Contemporary Christians must exercise the same vigor and enthusiasm embodied in the old spiritual:

> I keep so busy praising my Savior,
> Keep so busy praising my Lord.
> If I don't praise Him
> The rocks gonna cry out
> Glory and Honor, Glory and Honor,
> I ain't got time to die.

Nothing should get in the way of singing God's praises. This presumes that we be willing to surrender to the worship process. For when we surrender, we are in fact subordinating ourselves to the worship and service of God, as we are drawn into a sensitivity to his presence through the workings of the Holy Spirit. This sensitivity awakens us to the contributions and needs of other worship participants and forces us to sacrifice our own egos so that the church as a whole may be successful in glorifying God and ministering to the needs of the hurting.

Prayer is vital to this process. The Word of God tells us that Paul and Silas prayed and sang praises to God. Prayer is essential to an effective music ministry. Prayer moves the focus from self to God. It creates a sincerity that invites God to commune with us at the tables of our hearts. The words of Jesus to the Samaritan woman at the well hold special meaning: "For it is not where we worship that counts, but how we worship—is our worship spiritual and real? Do we have the Holy Spirit's help? For God is Spirit, and we must have his help to worship as we should" (John 4:23-24, TLB).

Our worship must be spiritual and real and must be guided by the Holy Spirit. God must be the focus and not we ourselves. Therefore, we must approach worship humbly and sincerely; and as we ready for church on Sunday morning, we should be able to say like the elders, "I woke up this morning with my mind stayed on Jesus."

The prison worship of Paul and Silas was spiritually real as it prepared them for the coming moments when they would be used as God's instruments for ministry.

The text clearly informs us that the other prisoners could hear Paul and Silas singing; however, the text is not so clear in sharing with us the effect the singing had on them.

The full results of our witness will not always be apparent either. We may never know how many lonely hearts we have comforted nor will there always be a visible gauge to indicate how many prisoners of sin shall find freedom in Christ as a result of our witness. Yet, it is important that we still sing praises to God. By singing God's praises, we provide ministry to his people; and he will provide the increase.

It is also important to notice that Paul and Silas did not limit their praise singing to the confines of the church community. They sang praises while in jail in the company of convicted criminals. Our music ministry should not be restricted to church buildings but should take us out into the hedges and highways. We should take our songs to jails, rest homes, and other types of secular settings.

These songs of praise should be used to evangelize souls, to bring faith to the disheartened and hope to the disinherited. Through song, we can minister to those who are despondent and sorrowful. Through hymns of healing, we can tell them that:

> There is a balm in Gilead to
> make the wounded whole;
> There is a balm in Gilead
> to heal the sin-sick soul.

For Paul and Silas, these songs also served as anthems for action. For, when the earthquake shook the foundation of the prison and loosened the bonds of the prisoners, Paul and Silas found themselves in perfect position to act as ambassadors for Christ. They acted quickly by ministering to the jailer who was on the verge of suicide. The jailer's sudden despondency resulted from a fear of the consequences facing him for losing his assigned prisoners. Paul prevented the suicide by assuring the jailer that none of the prisoners had escaped.

Then, in obedience to the Great Commission, Paul informed the jailer that, if he would believe on the Lord Jesus Christ, he would be saved.

We, too, should allow our songs of praise to prepare us for Christian action. These songs should arouse us so that we may help someone in need or lead someone to Christ. These songs should inspire us to act against the forces of iniquity and injustice; for, in the aftermath of our story, Paul and Silas demanded the justice guaranteed them as citizens of Rome.

In recent history, Black Americans have adopted the glorious tradition of Paul and Silas by singing God's praises as anthems for action. Like Paul in Rome, they have demanded the justice due them—first, as human beings during the slave era—and, later, as citizens of this land. Throughout the ceaseless struggle for liberation, songs of praise have called Black people to action. Historian E. Franklin Frazier speaks of the manifestations of this song tradition during the Civil Rights movement:

> As Negro students go forth singing the spirituals or the Gospel hymns when they engage in sit down strikes or sing their Gospel songs in response to violence, they are behaving in accordance with the religious heritage of the Negro.

As we serve in the 1980s, our songs of praise should call us to action, for there is meaning in the hymn "A Charge to keep I have, A God to glorify . . . To serve this present age, My calling to fulfill."

In this era of nuclear arms build-up, we should sing "Let there be peace on earth and let it begin with me" In this age of racial disharmony, we should sing "In Christ there is no East or West, In him no South or North; But one great fellowship of love Thro'out the whole wide earth." In this day when Christian people turn their backs on the poor and homeless, our song should be a reminder that when we deny the least of our brethren, we deny Christ, for "Away in a manger, no crib for a bed, The little Lord Jesus laid down his sweet head."

Finally, we learn from Paul and Silas that the end result of singing

God's praises is victory. For, in the end, Paul and Silas were released from prison. God had delivered them from the den of suffering.

Therefore, we must convey to God's people that suffering is just the first stanza in the song of victory, while the last stanza rings forth as a psalm of salvation. "Weeping may endure for a night, but joy cometh in the morning" (Ps. 30:5). Yes, Jesus suffered on Calvary and lay dead on that dark sabbath night. But when the morning came, Jesus walked out of the tomb, causing songs of joy to fill the spiritual airs of eternity.

That is why I cannot contain my joy each time I hear Sister Billie Poole and the Allen Temple Choir sing that great gospel song, "God Is!" This song testifies:

> God is the joy and strength of my life.
> He moves all pain, misery and strife.
> He promised to keep me, never to leave me.
> He never comes short of His word.

The song also offers a personal commitment as it proclaims:

> I want to go with Him, when He goes back
> I've gone too far and I can't turn back
> God is! God is! God is my All and All!

The proclamation "God Is" is a testimony that we have in Christ which embodies my very own praise experience with God. I praise him because he comforts me during my dark hours of pain. I praise him because he promised the faithful a wonderful home, where "the wicked will cease from troubling; and there the weary be at rest" (Job 3:17). All because God is! God is real! His promise is real! His works are real! His love is real! And his victory is real! He is real ontologically, existentially, and morally! He responds to our songs of hope by knocking down the prison doors of sin and death and liberating our souls to eternity! Because of his victory, we can continue to sing processionals of praises, hymns of healing, anthems for action, and psalms of salvation!

A Message Which Helped to Shape a Life
Charles Satchell Morris, II

" *'Nobility Brings Obligations* (Noblesse Oblige)' *I heard for the first time in May 1949 at Tennessee A & I State University, Nashville, at the National 4-H Convocation. It was fortunate for me to have heard this message when I was just fifteen years old because it did much to shape my thoughts as a youth,"* asserted Dr. *Edward Victor Hill, now minister in the Mount Zion Baptist Church, Los Angeles, referring to this address delivered by Dr. Charles Satchell Morris, II, twice a professor of English in that institution.*

Among other persons Dr. Morris taught here are President Walter S. Davis; Dr. Granville Sawyer, former president of Texas Southern University, Houston; Mrs. Josie Bain, highest-ranking Black executive with the Los Angeles Board of Education; Cecil Partee, now speaker pro tem of the Illinois State Senate; Judges Billy Jones of East Saint Louis; Luther T. Clanton, Jr., Des Moines; Charles Farmer, Detroit; A. Lincoln James, minister in the Bethesda Baptist Church, Chicago, and his brother, Samuel H. James, minister in the Second Baptist Church, San Antonio and councilman in that city; Odie Hoover, pastor of the huge Olivet Institutional Baptist Church, Cleveland, Ohio; also, President Levi Watkins of Alabama State University.

In view of the tremendous impact of this message upon persons across the nation, Dr. Brent has urged Dr. Morris to publish a synopsis of this address. Dr. Morris has served in eight college professorships where he had marvelous influence. As minister in the Bethel Baptist Institutional Church, Jacksonville, Florida's oldest parish, he has been honored for his service by having his portrait hanging upon the wall. Thrice he has served as a United States government official. Here is the synopsis of "Nobility Brings Obligation" for the historical record.

Noblesse Oblige—Nobility Brings Obligations

The French have a phrase of which I am inordinately fond: *Noblesse Oblige,* which, roughly translated, means "nobility brings obligations." Today, it is a special privilege to return to this beauteous institution where twice I held professorships in yesteryear. This sloping hillside nestling coyly in the fond embrace of sylvan slopes has intrigued me ever.

I wish to develop my theme from two viewpoints: First, being what I am, there are certain things which I must not be; second, being what I am, there are certain things which I must be.

I Must not Be

I cannot afford to be frivolous. Being what I am, a student in the universe of God, I must be sincere, earnest, serious. This I can be without being solemn. Someone has said that it requires seventy-two muscles to frown, but just eight to smile. With cheerfulness and kindly countenance, approach your tasks. The question once was asked whether a frivolous person, termed a jitterbug, was a man or an animal. The reply was that he was a man who acted like an animal but was far less dignified. Even the horse and cow have innate grace; the dog and cat, symmetry.

I cannot afford to be haughty. I should know so little that I do not know that I do not know. In fact, some wise men have gone beyond that, discovering that they did not even know that they did not know. Josh Billings observed that the trouble with most people is not that they do not know but that they know so many things that "ain't" so. The venerable Black preacher had been ridiculed by the young people of his congregation returning from college with haughty mien. One Sunday night, before a crowded church, he determined to get even. So he shouted, "I'll fix you, you A. B.'s—you African baboons; you A. M.'s—you American monkeys; you B. S.'s—you Black scamps!" probably with some justification. For haughtiness consists primarily in looking down upon others. You should be looking up with the others. For there not only are many down and outers, there are just as many up and outers.

I cannot afford to be unjust. If the world owes you a living, then you certainly owe the world a life. The purpose of the school and the college is not to reform but to form. If you entered crooked and perverse, you probably will depart more definitely so. Someone has said that an ignorant person who has thieving propensities will probably steal coal from the railroad. Educated, he probably will steal the railroad itself. Ignorant, he will steal a postage stamp; educated, he will attempt to steal the post office. Whereas in one's untrained state one will steal by retail, educated, without being disciplined in character, one will steal by wholesale.

I cannot afford to be ungrateful. Shakespeare declared that ingratitude in a child is sharper than a serpent's tooth or venom. Each one of us is a debtor to everyone of us. To our associates, friends, to mankind generally, but especially to God. No man is an island; no man lives alone; all that we put into the lives of others will come back into our own. The world is demanding of educated young men and women either a reasonable service or a reason that is serviceable. You should live lives of thanks since that is the best way to show thanksgiving. I must enlarge the horizons of my own mind and increase the diameter of my own heart, extend the periphery of my own soul. Since I must spend most of my time with myself, I wish to be on friendly terms with my own spirit. The lawyer thanked the grouchy and sour elevator operator and his friend remonstrated: "Why do you thank an old sourpuss like that?"

"I thanked him not because of the kind of man he is, but because of the kind of man I am."

I cannot afford to be prejudiced. Edwin Markham exultantly sings:

> He drew a circle and shut me out—
> Heretic, rebel, a thing to flout.
> But Love and I had the wit to win:
> We drew a circle that took him in.

God has endowed all of us with the capacity to enjoy, with a brain to function—had he desired a White man to think for me, he would have placed a White head upon a Black body—with a heart to love and a soul to sing. I must not be prejudiced against myself; I must be able to forgive and forget the many mistakes of yesterday. I must not be prejudiced against men because of the accident of race or the choice of creed. I must not be prejudiced against great ideas and ideals which lift the minds of men toward the sunlit summits. And certainly I must not be prejudiced against God from whom all blessings flow. For I still revel in the trembling events of that frantic, frenetic Friday when he died that I might live forever.

I Must Be

Then, turning briefly to the second phase of my theme, I wish to urge that there are certain things which I must do and be.

I must be loyal to myself. I cannot be loyal unless I am true; and, if I am true to myself and I happen to be false, then, in the final analysis, I am disloyal. I cannot separate myself from the stream of history and be a hermit. I shall be compelled to make choices. Some young people take the high road and some take the low. There is an hour of decision for every young person and that hour may determine your fate. Do not touch alcohol or narcotics for the first time and you never will have to fight these imposters thereafter. Dr. E. Stanley Jones points out, in that marvelous book *The Christ of the Indian Road*, that you must at times make a decision. If you put off, defer, delay, decide to wait, you already have made a decision not to decide; and that, in itself, is a decision. To decide not to decide is indecision, and that may be the final decision. "This one thing I do" said the immortal Paul in an ecstatic outburst of finality.

I must be loyal to humanity. Wordsworth sings of its still, sad music. Another poet reminds us that heard things are sweet, but those unheard are sweeter. Robert Browning reminds us in *Saul:* "'Tis not what man Does which exalts him, but what man Would do." Service is the rent we pay for the space which we occupy. If we do not serve humanity, then we are not paying our rent for our presence in this world. We gather in our churches to worship: we depart to serve. Members of this National 4-H organization, go forth to bury yourselves in order that others may live and you will live afresh in them. Give away so much of yourselves that you give yourselves away. Give of your time, your money, your talent.

> Not what we give, but what we share,
> The gift without the giver is bare;
> Who gives himself with his alms feeds three,—
> Himself, his hungering neighbor, and me.

I must be loyal to truth. God securely locked his laws in the vault of the universe before he bade time race through marvelous mountains, flecky clouds, verdant valleys, trembling trees, or shimmering snow. "What is truth?" asked Pilate and would not stay for an answer. Truth is that which is. It is eternal, unalterable, unequivocal. Everything must either be or not be. Nothing can both be and not be. There is analysis, thesis, and sythesis. "No teacher or master may decide for me what is good, but in my own soul must the decision be made," exultantly sang the philosophical Ralph Waldo Emerson. "Poetry," declared Grenville Keiser, "is the smile upon the face of truth," and its laws emanate from the being of God. Unfettered, my mind must be, for it to me a kingdom is. The sweetest cup of tea is the cup of liberty. "What kind of bug is this?" queried the students of the wise old professor of biology when ingeniously they had assembled the antenna of a mosquito, the mouth of a fly, the stinger of a bee, the fluorescence of a lightning bug. A quick examination ensued and then he announced, "Why, young gentlemen, that is a humbug."

For He who worketh wise and good,
Nor errs within His plan,
Will take the sun out of the skies,
Ere freedom out of man.

In the sunlit sanctum of truth, error will flee as mist fades before the regal rays of the succulent summer's sun.

I must be loyal to the quest for knowledge. Its acquisition is not a bequest; but, like liberty, is a conquest. God takes ninety days to grow a squash but a century to rear an oak to sweep the skies. Most freethinkers are free from thinking. Often during yesteryear when I was dubious concerning the preparation of some of my students in this institution, I inquired as to whether they had studied the lesson. To which they often replied: "Well, Professor, we looked over the assignment," to which I rejoined, "Well, you seem to have overlooked it."

You can learn everywhere. Lessons in courtesy and chivalry you may often learn from folk the world designates as ignorant. You can learn from a lisping, prattling babe, from hoary, hairy age, from the wise, and from the foolish. The Bible declares that men are saved through the foolishness of preaching. There is a difference between that and foolish preaching.

The student examining the examination questions in a certain course at the end of the first quarter in the college in which he had matriculated and not recognizing even one the answer to which he was able to supply wrote this at the bottom of the sheet: "Only God knows the answer to these questions. Merry Christmas!" The professor in due season received and examined the paper. Like the student, he had a sudden inspiration for he appended this reply: "God gets *A,* you get *F.* Happy New Year!" God always will get *A,* but you should not always get *F.*

Finally, *I must be loyal to high ideals.* Shakespeare asserted that: "Finds tongues in trees, books in the running brooks, Sermons in stones, and good in every thing." If you dedicate your lives to high ideals, you will increase the force and momentum thereof, but what is far more important you will enlarge the horizons of your own hearts and souls. Three men are working on a monumental structure. One, asked what he was doing, said, "I am making five dollars a day." The second said, "I am working at my trade as a stonemason." The third responded, "I am building a cathedral."

Ideals are motivated ideas. People supply the motivation. The idea is timeless and in the heart of God. "Every man has a John Brown in his soul," wrote Ralph Waldo Emerson when the greatest of American Abolitionists had been hanged from a gallows in hideous Charlestown jail. "But he made that gallows glorious like unto the cross." An idea raises a sleek, streamlined ship to swim in the stratospheric zeniths supreme beyond the feathered tribes. An idea transformed a savage into a saint through the grace of God. An idea displaced a sailboat, enabling mighty monarchs of the ocean to glide through stellar space. Invention and discovery. The greatest invention of eternity was that of the plan of salvation whereby God enable man to become a member of the "royal family." The greatest discovery of the ages is not that of Niagara or Victoria Falls or of the Mississippi River or the Pacific Ocean, but when man discovers God for himself. Young people, dedicate yourself to the highest and the best. Walk with him who suspended the sun across the archway of the heavens and whose light illumines our souls as we walk through the exacting, eroding earth in which we live. For, as Rudyard Kipling, England's sweet singer, saw momentarily the deathless, dramatic, delightful dream:

> When earth's last picture is painted.
> And the tubes are twisted and dried,
> When the oldest colours have faded,
> and the youngest critic has died,
> We shall rest, and, faith we shall need it—
> lie down for an aeon or two,
> Till the Master of All Good Workmen,
> Shall put us to work anew,
> Then those that were good shall be happy:
> they shall sit in a golden chair;
> They shall splash at a ten-league canvas,
> with brushes of comets' hair,
>
> They shall find real saints to draw from—
> Magdalene, Peter, and Paul;
> They shall work for an age at a sitting,
> and never be tired at all!
>
> And only the Master shall praise us,
> and only the Master shall blame;
> And no one shall work for money,
> and no one shall work for fame,
> But each for the joy of the working,
> and each in his separate star,
> Shall draw the Thing as he sees It,
> For the God of Things as They Are.